THE SECRET WORLD OF
CULTS

THE SECRET WORLD OF
CULTS

FROM ANCIENT DRUIDS
TO HEAVEN'S GATE

Sarah Moran

Bramley Books

Project Editor • Suzanne Evins
Design • Peter Laws
Jacket Design • Philip Chidlow
Design Manager • Justina Leitão
Picture Research • Christine Cornick
Copyeditor • Huw Jones
Production • Neil Randles and Karen Staff

5113 The Secret World of Cults

Published in 1999 by Bramley Books, an imprint of Quadrillion Publishing Ltd,

Godalming Business Centre, Woolsack Way, Godalming, Surrey GU7 1XW, England.

ISBN 1-84100-132-5

Printed and bound in Italy by New Interlitho SpA

AUTHOR'S ACKNOWLEDGMENTS

It is impossible to list all the books, articles and indeed people that have helped with the research for this book. I have done my best to give due credit to other authors and researchers, whose in-depth knowledge of specific areas or groups has been invaluable.

Another excellent source of information has been the Internet, and I would certainly recommend that anyone who is interested in carrying out further research makes the most of this relatively new resource. Many of the groups I have written about have their own World Wide Web home pages, and there are countless other sites devoted to the subject of cults. The lack of censorship on the Internet allows open debate, presenting arguments both for and against individual cults, and this gives a unique insight into what remains a very controversial topic.

Many thanks to everyone who has helped with this book. Special thanks must go to Huw and Christine for all their hard work, and of course to Sue for keeping everything going remarkably smoothly and giving me valuable advice. A big hug to David for reading through the manuscript, despite it being "not really my thing," and most of all, to Ian, who, quite simply, I adore.

CONTENTS

INTRODUCTION

THE WIDELY ACCEPTED DEFINITION of a "cult" is a group of individuals who share a set of religious or quasi-religious beliefs, often imposed by a charismatic leader, which tend not to conform to society's norms, and may be considered fanatical. Many groups which fit this definition now prefer the less contentious title of "new religious movement," because over the last fifty years the word "cult" has become linked with brainwashing, mass suicide, and even murder.

Cults are not a new phenomenon, and they have always attracted controversy. Throughout history, humanity has formed secret societies and secular groups to try to make sense of the world. Most of the time, their strong beliefs have sprung from dissatisfaction with mainstream religions, although the influence of Christianity, Hinduism, and Buddhism can be seen in many of today's cults. Ancient cults such as the Knights Templar and Rosicrucians also had links to Christianity, but their secretive ceremonies and allegiance to powerful leaders set them apart from the rest of society.

Despite popular preconceptions, a cult need not necessarily be a destructive group. It has often been pointed out that Christianity was itself once a cult, so it is possible that some present-day cults will be accepted as mainstream religions in the future. For example, in the USA, Mormonism is nowadays seen as a respectable and genuine religious movement, and its members are so highly regarded that they are actively recruited by government organizations like the FBI, but the group did originate as a cult, and some of its beliefs are anything but mainstream.

Much depends on the qualities of the "charismatic leader," if there is one. A dictatorial cult leader is as potentially dangerous as a dictatorial political leader, perhaps even more so, because members are subjected to their guru's every whim—often portrayed as being inspired by some form of "higher power"—and are told that they will only reach salvation if they obey his or her every word.

Destructive cults are not only dangerous for their individual members, but for society as a whole. At the most extreme are cults like the Japanese Aum Supreme Truth, which foresaw a new world order brought about by a chemical and biological war which was to be instigated by their own members. On a lesser scale, membership of a cult such as the Moonies will also have repercussions in wider society, even if it is just the severing of family ties.

While some cults can be said to hold views outside the norms of society, they don't necessarily pose a threat to members of the wider community. Cults such as the modern Druids do follow leaders and hold special ceremonies, but they work to

improve the environment for everybody, and membership doesn't involve rejecting society's entire value system. However, other cults, especially those that have gained notoriety over the years, often started out with a belief system that many would consider only marginally different to the norm, but under the influence of various infamous gurus, spiraled out of control when power, sex, and money were introduced into the equation.

A relatively new phenomenon in the world of cults is the growth of the Militia movement and the far right in the USA. These groups, such as the Posse Comitatus and Michigan Militia, display some classic similarities with other types of cults. They generally have a charismatic leader, they have a definite belief system, and many of them base their ideas on a form of fundamentalist Christianity. Their numbers are growing for the same reason that numbers of certain other cults are increasing—because of a feeling that mainstream society is failing them.

People join cults for a variety of reasons. The popularity of so-called "accepted" religions is dwindling, and the interest in mysticism, new age teachings and the occult is certainly growing. Particularly in the West, where spirituality has been eclipsed by the joys of wealth and material gratification, more and more people seem to be looking for a spiritual aspect to their lives. If mainstream religion fails to supply this, then there are numerous cults around which appear to promise either guaranteed salvation, or at least a close-knit community of like-minded friends.

11

There are now many anti-cult groups which produce literature warning of the dangers of cult membership, and also many ex-members who have written accounts of their time in a cult. Some, but not all, would argue that their lives have become more fulfilled by joining a cult, and that their beliefs and way of life are as valid as anybody else's.

Cultwatch groups have identified specific types of people who are more likely to be targeted by recruiters. Young people seem to be particularly susceptible—when you're on the verge of having to make life-altering decisions, it is often easier to be given an identity than to forge one for yourself. Groups such as the UK-based INFORM and the American Cult Awareness Network believe they can recognize a pattern in the recruiting techniques, initiation programs, and fundraising activities of most cults, and they tour schools and colleges, informing young people about different cults' recruiting techniques, and alerting them to potential dangers.

Today, cults continue to generate much criticism among the media, which has led to some claiming that their members are persecuted, and others going as far as suing for damages. But these groups and their extraordinary leaders are bound to attract publicity—indeed, some court it—and this is likely to be adverse when their beliefs are practiced in such a way that they not only contradict society's norms, but are sometimes illegal.

Chapter One

SECRET SOCIETIES

THE SEARCH FOR ANCIENT WISDOM

OUR IMPRESSIONS OF THE ACTIVITIES of secretive societies from our past are often colored by romanticism and an idealized view of history, but many had sinister beginnings, and still have an influence today. It is important to maintain a balance between paranoid conspiracy theories, which see a world dominated to this day by corrupt and powerful groups such as the Illuminati and the Freemasons, and a naive refusal to believe that the cults discussed in this chapter have ever wielded great influence.

It is little wonder that these secretive organizations which believe they hold the key to a "new world order," or at least to the problems of contemporary life, have been treated with suspicion. Examining not only the history, but the modern influences of these groups can give us an insight into part of Western history that has for too long remained a secret, only revealed to those who knew passwords, handshakes, and secret meeting places. In some cases, the influence of these organizations is apparent in society today—indeed, some could be said to have the potential to change the course of modern history.

Whether they be the now-peaceful Druids or the highly contentious Freemasons, it is important to understand what goes on behind their closed doors. Many more dangerous groups have started out in a similar way to these historic societies, believing they have something special that the rest of society either can't know about or doesn't understand. Are they just forward-thinking organizations working toward what they believe will benefit mankind, or are their motives less honorable?

Throughout history the search for the meaning of life has intrigued not only radical thinkers, but ordinary people intent on broadening their horizons. Secret knowledge, such as alchemy, was the basis for a number of clandestine organizations.

THE KNIGHTS TEMPLAR

In 1099, the Christian soldiers of the Crusades captured Jerusalem from the Arabs. It wasn't a definitive triumph, though, and the Holy City had to be constantly protected from attacks by the "infidel." The Christians saw the crusades as a Holy War, and indeed had backing, both philosophical and financial, from the Pope. Because of this, some of the fighting factions were ordained monks. One of the most famous of these religious orders was the Order of the Knights Templar, a group of highly trained fighters who pledged their lives to defending the Holy Land.

The Order is still shrouded in mystery, and accounts of its activities have always been conflicting. They have been linked with Satanism, the search for the Holy Grail, the Illuminati, and modern-day Free-masonry. It is also possible that the spirit of the Order is still maintained even today.

Hughes de Paynes, a French nobleman, founded his order of pious knights around 1118. Initially a group of just nine devout men who pledged a vow of poverty and brotherhood, it was only when the group was granted a blessing by the Pope the following year that it started attracting new followers. By 1128, when the Order was given its own set of "rules" for monastic life, the Knights Templar were already an influential mix of noblemen, landowners, and businessmen.

The Order decreed that all personal wealth must be signed over on joining, and it quickly amassed lands all over Europe, as well as great wealth and influence. The daily life of the Knights was one of strict religious servitude, which now seems strangely at odds with their deserved reputation for being highly skilled warriors. They were also well known for bravery, and were allegedly forbidden to flee from a battlefield unless

The Knights Templar covered their chainmail armor with long cloaks decorated with the red Templar cross—a fitting outfit for the "soldiers of Christ."

outnumbered by three to one. Over 20,000 Templars are thought to have died for their Pope.

The Knights grew extremely powerful, establishing Templar enclaves that resembled small, autonomous states in England, Scotland, Germany, France, Spain, and various other European countries. Each headquarter was presided over by a Master who was directly answerable to the Grand Master in Jerusalem. Their wealth and intimacy with the Pope meant they wielded important influence within the European courts—influence which would, in the end, lead to their downfall.

As the initial vow, to protect every Christian in the Crusades, was gradually obscured, their activities also became less noble. Money-lending on a grand scale was rife, even to the extent that King Henry III of England had to pawn the crown jewels to the Templars for six years! Templars were renowned for being good businessmen, running ship-yards, hospitals, and financial institu-tions, and were at the forefront of new technologies, both scientific and medical. Rumors started that the Order was colluding with the enemy, if not directly, then by at least lending money to them, and there is some evidence that concessions were made between the Order in Jerusalem and some of its Muslim neighbors. While the Pope began to worry about the extent of the Order's power, someone else had decided enough was enough.

King Philip IV of France had often relied on Templar monies, and even housed some of his treasury in Templar buildings. The Knights were secretive and discreet, which suited his needs, and their specially constructed round forts were very safe. However, he became convinced the Knights wanted to overthrow him and establish themselves as rulers of France. He had grand plans to

An ancient temple at Laon, France, that has a long association with the persecuted Order of Knights. It has the typical rounded design of Templar churches.

ADMISSIONS OF GUILT

The Templars were subjected to the torture instruments of the Church's Inquisition, and what followed was a list of abominations and heresies that, according to the Pope, were punishable by death. How true these allegations were is still open to debate, but nevertheless, with the insistence of the Pope, kings all over Europe began to persecute the once respected Order.

The Knights were imprisoned in harsh conditions, and subjected to torture until they admitted the Order had carried out a long list of blasphemous actions.

The initiation rites of the Order proved central to the Inquisition's accusations. According to signed confessions, Masters had organized darkened rituals where homosexual acts were performed, Christ was denounced, and Christian symbols were defaced. A bizarre ritual of

"obscene kisses" was supposed to have been performed by new recruits. By candlelight, the initiate would be expected to kiss his master's lips, stomach and genitals—a ritual with distinctly Satanic overtones.

In addition to these darker practices, the allegedly devout Order of warrior monks was also accused of worshiping a "false idol." The name Baphomet recurred in various confessions, some not induced by torture. Some also spoke of worshiping a "head"—a statue of a man's face with long hair and a Christ-like beard. Many researchers have speculated as to what Baphomet could have been. Some believe it is the secret of the Holy Grail—the true whereabouts of the body of Christ and the sacred knowledge of His bloodline.

A SACRED SEAL

16

The Order of the Knights Templar retained the same symbol from its very beginnings as a simple Order of nine knights vowed to poverty and defense of the Christians in the Holy Land. To represent poverty, two knights are depicted riding the same horse. The seal became a symbol of high finance, even guaranteeing that loans agreed by one country's Templar headquarters would be paid on arrival at another's.

The monks themselves wore large, blood-red crosses on their robes, and also decorated the outside of their buildings with the same sign. Not only did this make them recognizable, for they were extremely proud of the elevated status the Order gave them, but their buildings were then exempt from taxation. However, this simple marking proved problematic in certain English towns when local people started painting the sacred cross on their own buildings to avoid paying taxes.

take over Europe, and was in serious need of funds, so destroying the grip of the respected Knights would bring several benefits. He began to plot their downfall.

In October 1307, King Philip instructed his troops to storm Templar buildings and arrest those found within for questioning. Friends had forewarned some Templars with connections in court, but others were caught by surprise. The Grand Master, Jacques de Molay, was arrested along with 60 others on the night of October 12th 1307. Molay was to be the last Grand Master of the

TEMPLAR KNIGHTS CONFESSED TO SPITTING ON THE CRUCIFIX AND WORSHIPING FALSE IDOLS

Order. He was burnt at the stake, shouting his innocence and retracting his forced confessions before the assembled crowds.

The Pope, Clement V, was reportedly in the pay of Philip. He had tried to calm the Inquisition initially, but felt he was in a delicate position, so when Philip publicized the confessions and French popular opinion seemed to be behind him, the Pope gave his consent for the tortures to continue.

A stream of accusations were leveled against the captured Knights Templar, all men who felt they had been loyal to both their God and their respective countries. It was standard practice to read the same list of charges to those being tortured, so when more than one Templar knight confessed to urinating on the cross, worshiping false idols or indecent kisses, this was taken as confirmation that the activities had taken place.

Torture was only used in France or in French-ruled countries, until the Pope intervened. Of 138 Templars "questioned" in Paris between October and November 1307, 36 were said to have died, and 123 confessed to the least offensive charge of spitting on the crucifix during ceremonies. This was understandable considering the torture methods adopted by the Inquisition, the favorite of which, according to John J. Robinson in his book *Dungeon, Fire and Sword*, was: "an iron frame like a bed, on which the Templar was strapped with his bare feet hanging over the end. A charcoal brazier was slid under his oiled feet as the questioning began. Several Knights were reported to have gone mad with the pain. A number had their feet totally burnt off." It is testimony to the Templars' faith that only three of the 138 admitted to the homosexual practices that Philip so wanted to use to discredit the organization. While the monarch had success in France, and the Order lost its popular support, other countries weren't keen to punish the group.

Those Templars who recanted their confessions were burnt, but those who maintained their admissions of guilt were set free—admittedly with severe physical and psychological wounds, and into a life of poverty.

In England and Scotland, torture wasn't used at first, and although the respective authorities eventually

Above: Two Templars standing behind a single shield on the western facade of Chartres Cathedral in France.

Left: A depiction of the knights in monks' garb being arrested and led into prison, ready for questioning.

rounded up the Templars in 1308, when the Pope ordered all Christian nations to arrest the Order, most were allowed to escape. Other European countries announced that they couldn't find the Order guilty of anything either, so the Pope sent in the Inquisition. Even under torture, nothing of use was gained from the English Templars, and most survived the experience, fleeing to Scotland, a country which had always valued their presence.

According to Desmond Seward in *The Monks of War*, writing about Paris, "by the end of May [1310], 120 Templars had been burnt." In England, only four out of more than two hundred admitted spitting on the cross.

While conventional history records the early 1300s as being the end for the group of warrior knights known as the Templars, others have collected pieces of a vast jigsaw that makes the story a lot less simple. The Knights Templar may have had links to the Priory of Sion, the ancient organization which still exists, charged with protecting the bloodline of Jesus. More than one researcher has found links between the founding of the Templar Knights in 1118 and the Priory. Although the Order professed to be in the Holy Land to protect its fellow Christians, Gaetan Delaforge, in *The Templar Tradition in the Age of Aquarius*, speculates: "the real task of the nine knights was to carry out research in the area in order to obtain certain relics and manuscripts ... some of which went back to the days of Moses."

More recently, author Graham Hancock, in *The Sign and the Seal*, suggested it was "highly probable that Hugh de Paynes and his backer the Count of Champagne could ... have been motivated by a desire to find the Ark." If this was the case, then the Templars and the Priory would have both considered themselves true guardians of the world's most important secret, which would explain why the two groups are thought to have merged for a while, only splitting after the persecution and dissolution of the Knights Templar.

THE ROSICRUCIANS

The Rosicrucians are members of another secretive organization which is supposed to have forged links with the Knights Templar, the Freemasons, and the Illuminati. Certainly there are strong links with the Masons that survive until this day, the most obvious being that one of the Freemasons' highest degrees for initiates is mysteriously known as the Rose-Croix Degree.

The Ancient Mystical Order of the Rosy Cross, to give the group its full title, has similarities with the Knights Templar, although the members were never warriors, and its history is often intertwined with that of the doomed Order of Knights. It was officially recognized as an Order when three books were published during 1614–1616. The books document the life of a mythical Rosicrucian called Christian Rosenkreuz, who was said to have lived for 108 years, traveled the world, and spread the word about mystical learning. The books also stated that when Rosenkreuz's grave was discovered and exhumed in 1604, the body was perfectly intact, just as the bodies of some Christian saints were supposed to remain uncorrupted after death.

The books stirred up a new interest in the mysterious "religion," and many of the Renaissance's finest minds became involved with the secretive organization. The modern groups, of which there are many, trace the history of their movement back to the Egyptian Pharaohs, who developed an interest in "secret wisdom." Even today, the Order is preoccupied with the answers to mystical questions and concerned with freeing the soul through spiritual understanding. The Greeks are supposed to have brought back some of Egypt's secret teachings to the West. AMORC (The Ancient Mystical Order Rosae Crucis), the largest Rosicrucian order still operating, also says their history lies in the "highly advanced Arab

The Rosy Cross, the ancient symbol of the secretive order. The 22 petals of the Rose symbolize the 22 secret paths of the cabala, a mystical doctrine.

Civilization [which] preserved a large body of mystical teachings through texts translated directly from the great libraries of the ancient world."

The Arabs did have an advanced knowledge of science and medicines, which, together with their more mystical philosophies, was probably absorbed and brought back to Western Europe by travelers such as the Knights Templar. One of the major fascinations of the Rosicrucians was science, in particular alchemy, and many of the best-known alchemists belonged to the Order of the Rosy Cross. Count Saint Germain, who had links to both the Illuminati and the Rosicrucians as well as being a confidante of Marie Antoinette, claimed to have found the Philosopher's Stone, which would give him eternal life as well as bestow all the secrets of alchemy on him. He is alleged to have appeared to various people over the centuries, most recently in the 1970s, when a Frenchman turned up claiming to be the Count. Saint Germain has been ranked alongside the supposedly mystical character of Christian Rosenkreuz by the Theosophical Society, who claim the two are part of a council of Grand Masters waiting to share their spiritual knowledge with the world.

Today, the Rosicrucian movement is most popular in the USA, and it is estimated that there are approximately 200,000 students, with an unknown number of fully initiated followers. Some groups still maintain their secrecy, which dates back to the times when such mystical societies were either banned or persecuted, but AMORC is very open about itself, even advertising home study courses for beginners. The teachings are still based on a Gnostic form of Christianity, which means a complex study of mysticism through the ages, hopefully leading to a source of inner strength for the individual.

AMORC operates a system of progression through the

*A*MORC's modern research center, Rosicrucian Park, at their San Jose headquarters in California, is decorated with Ancient Egyptian symbolism.

ALCHEMY

QUEST FOR ETERNAL LIFE

The study of alchemy has fascinated people right up to the present day. The Arabs believed that the Egyptians had somehow discovered how to turn base metals into gold, so detailed and prolific was their work in the precious metal. Aristotle's basic philosophy that everything on earth was made from a mixture of the four elements—earth, fire, water, and air—led to the beginnings of scientific research, and although all manner of advances have been made, the fascination with alchemy continues.

As romanticism and radical philosophy mixed with basic scientific practices, the elusive element that the alchemist needed was termed the "Philosopher's Stone." It was generally believed, even by scientific minds such as Descartes and Newton (both of whom became involved with the Order of the Rosy Cross), that the Philosopher's Stone wouldn't just produce gold, but would hold the secret to eternal life, or at least longevity.

Rosicrucians believe that the study of ancient mysticism will lead to individual enlightenment, and the Order is still surrounded by symbolism, most of which can be traced back to the early alchemists.

SOME GROUPS STILL MAINTAIN SECRECY FROM THE TIMES WHEN THEY WERE PERSECUTED

ranks via various initiations, in a manner very similar to the practice of the Masons. It even calls local groups of Rosicrucians "lodges." Although smaller groups can be set up locally for the benefit of students, only the Lodge can carry out the "inspiring Degree initiation rituals." Three Degrees must be obtained via the home study course first before progress can be made to obtain the further Lodge Degrees.

With ancient symbolism such as the gold equilateral triangle figuring in all Rosicrucian ceremonies, it is easy to see how closely the movement is linked to other ancient secretive orders. Some conspiracy theorists believe the Rosicrucians are yet another branch of the controversial Illuminati.

*S*aunière, the secretive priest, constructed an isolated library tower, Château Bethany, high up overlooking the French countryside.

THE PRIORY OF SION

The history of the secretive organization known as the Prieure du Sion is filled with mystery, intrigue, and many unanswered questions. If certain speculations about the organization—which still exists—are true, then its role is one of extreme importance and honor, but the story reads like an Indiana Jones adventure, with buried treasure, murders, cryptic codes, and frustrated historians. The case of the Priory of Sion and the mystery surrounding the French village of Rennes-le-Château is a wonderful example of fact being stranger than fiction.

A priest called Berenger Saunière was sent to the small village of Rennes-le-Château in 1885. He was charged with renovating the church and ministering to the local Catholic population. It was well known that he was poor, so when he started spending large sums of money on his church, other building work, and himself, people became suspicious. It seems that in 1891 Saunière found various old documents hidden under the altar of the church. How many he found is still disputed, but it is thought that two were documents recording the lineage of important families which dated from 1244 and 1644, and others

contained a series of secret codes. Saunière allegedly needed help translating the secret messages that are thought to have been left by the previous priest, but eventually the first was revealed to contain the message: "THIS TREASURE BELONGS TO DAGOBERT II KING AND TO SION AND HE IS THERE DEAD." According to Steve Mizrach's *The Mysteries of Rennes-le-Château and the Prieure du Sion*, another of the codes apparently contained the sentence: "SHEPHERDESS NO TEMPTATION THAT POUSSIN TENIERS HOLD THE KEY PEACE 681 BY THE CROSS AND THIS HORSE OF GOD I COMPLETE (DESTROY) THIS DAEMON GUARDIAN AT MIDDAY BLUE APPLES."

Further mysteries followed, including Saunière's refusal to expose how he was getting his money. He also completed the restoration of the church with some strange and unusual "clues." There is an effigy of a devilish creature, possibly the "daemon guardian" mentioned by the strange code. Many notable researchers have speculated that Saunière became privy to some information that it paid him well to keep quiet. He may have been resorting to blackmail.

Writers such as Michael Baigent, Richard Leigh, and Henry Lincoln believe that Saunière was linked to the Holy Grail. It was these three writers who made the link between the "Dagobert" mentioned in Saunière's code and King Dagobert II of the Merovingian dynasty which ruled Gaul (France) for over three hundred years. Steve Mizrach says: "the Merovingians were said to rule by right of their 'royal blood' or 'sang real.' 'Sangreal' has been traditionally interpreted as the 'holy grail' which, according to legend, Mary Magdalene carried to the Jewish kingdom of southern Gaul (including Rennes-le-Château)." These researchers suggest in their fascinating study, *The Holy Blood and the Holy Grail*, that the Holy Grail isn't in fact an object or the legendary treasure of Jerusalem, but that there is evidence to suggest that Jesus and Mary Magdalene were married, and Mary arrived in Gaul carrying their child—the child was the Holy Grail, and the secret of the Holy Grail is the secret of a direct bloodline from Christ.

It certainly seems an incredible story, and Baigent, Leigh, and Lincoln have uncovered links between the whole saga, the turbulent history of Europe, the

OTHER HIDDEN DOCUMENTS CONTAINED A SERIES OF SECRET CODES

Illuminati, the Masons, and the High Church. At the center of all this turmoil is a highly secretive society that still exists today—the Priory of Sion.

Headed up until 1984 by Pierre Plantard de St. Clair, who is allegedly himself linked to the Merovingian kings, the society maintains that it has an ancient lineage stretching back to Godfroi de Bouillion, who led the Knights Templar. Members have pledged to defend the right of the Merovingian dynasty and maintain its secrets until the time is right for them to be made public.

Obviously the claims of the secretive society could be nothing more than fantasy—especially as some of those linked with it have been among Europe's greatest writers and creative thinkers, such as Leonardo da Vinci, Isaac Newton, Victor Hugo, and Jean Cocteau—but the Order has been traced throughout history. Repeatedly, names linking it to certain noble and even royal families recur. The Priory is said to have had connections with the US government, top banking families, and the most notable freethinkers of each generation. They allegedly hope to create a United States of Europe and restore the true "sangreal" monarch to their rightful place.

21

THE TOMB OF JESUS

Some researchers, most recently Richard Andrews and Paul Schellenberger, have suggested that what Saunière's discovery points to, and what the Priory of Sion is actually protecting, is not the bloodline itself, but more simply the final burial place of Jesus's body. They suggest that a mountain near Rennes-le-Château could be what Saunière's mystical codes are actually referring to, and it is known that the Knights Templar formed a stronghold on the spot and were the only Templar group not persecuted by the French in the early 1300s. The site is also home to a legendary ancient Visigoth city, which ties all the grail links together very neatly.

The long-clawed "daemon guardian," created by Saunière, has an eerie presence within the church of Rennes-le-Château.

FREEMASONRY

Most Westerners are aware that a secret society of male-dominated "lodges" with links to local businesses exists. To some people, the idea of Freemasons prompts smiles and jokes about funny handshakes. To others the Freemasons are notable for their charitable works, especially for underprivileged children. The truth about the Freemasons and their history is a lot more complex than either preconception gives them credit for.

Freemasonry is probably the largest of all secret organizations today, and it is also very wealthy. The secrecy makes it difficult to establish their numbers, but it is thought that there are nearly 6 million fully initiated Freemasons world-wide.

The Catholic Church is particularly scathing of the movement. In 1738, Pope Clement XII, decreed that Catholics couldn't join the Freemasons, and any who did would face excommunication. Baptists are also discouraged from becoming involved with the movement, and it is banned in China, Greece, and some South American countries. Despite established religious figures damning their society as heretical and dangerous, Freemasons believe their ideals are tied closely to the Christian Church.

The movement has its roots in the English Middle Ages, where it was started as a trade union—a mutually beneficial organization for members of the itinerant building trade. The modern organization maintains the emphasis on helping fellow members in need, and many men join to further their business interests. Most lodges have recruited representatives of all the major professions.

When the building of churches and cathedrals began to slow down, the organization slowly disbanded, but it was revived in its present form in the eighteenth century, when a group of four lodges was created and bound together as the Grand Lodge of England in 1717.

The organization was molded into a secretive society rather than an open trade union, and exists in this way even today. A newcomer cannot ask to join, he must wait to be nominated, and a selection procedure follows.

Initiation ceremonies are said to range from the intricate to the bizarre, borrowing heavily on Rosicrucian and even occult practices. Although revealing the secrets of the Lodge is allegedly punishable by having your eyes gouged out, your bowel or heart ripped from your body, or removal of the tongue (practices that Masons say are purely symbolic), some ceremonial details have been made public.

In *A Book of Beliefs: Cults and New Faiths*, written by John Butterworth, the author gives an impressively detailed account of a Masonic initiation ritual. He describes the various stages a candidate must go through: for example, in stage one, after removing his jacket and tie, "his left trouser leg is then rolled up to his knee, his shirt is opened to expose his left breast and his right shoe is removed and replaced by a slipper." After the ceremonial disrobing, the initiate is blindfolded and made to wear a noose around his neck. The following stages involve swearing an oath of allegiance and swearing to secrecy. The secret handshake and signs are then

THE AMERICAN BROTHERHOOD

Freemasonry is very popular in the USA, with approximately three-quarters of all Masons being American. The movement was first established in Boston in 1733, and was set up under the patronage of the Grand Lodge of England. It flourished until a scandal in 1821 provoked a national outcry and the Anti-Masonic Party was formed. The scandal was the alleged kidnapping and murder of William Morgan, himself a Freemason, but one who had pledged to expose the secret rites of the group. It is thought that a group of Masons was responsible for his death, and the Anti-Masonic literature still makes much of the incident, using it as an example of Masonic corruption.

Right: The initiation of an apprentice in the 1890s.

Far right: The Temple Room of the Masonic Temple, Washington DC.

Below right: London's Grand Lodge opens its doors to the press for its 275th anniversary.

REVEALING LODGE SECRETS IS PUNISHABLE BY HAVING YOUR EYES GOUGED OUT

shown to the initiate so he will know how to recognize other Freemasons without revealing himself openly.

Masons say that all the practices are purely symbolic and are a sign of respect for the society's origins. They believe they can trace the Masons back further than the 1700s, to the Old Testament, where the builders of King Solomon's temple are said to have formed a lodge to protect their trade secrets from outsiders. Today, many Masonic symbols can be traced back to Ancient Egyptian symbols.

Despite its attempts to counter bad publicity with numerous good works, including funding of schools and hospitals, Freemasonry has continued to draw criticism from various sections of society. Many people believe the secretive nature of the brotherhood can only lead to corruption, especially when high-level offices in society such as judges, police commissioners, politicians, and clergy have all had representatives who were or are Masons. The code of practice which ensures a Mason never informs on another Mason, even when illegal activity is involved, has led to some embarrassing scandals, particularly within the legal profession.

Perhaps the greatest of all conspiracies to be linked to the movement is the infamous case of Jack the Ripper, the Victorian killer (or killers) of prostitutes in London. More than one historian has linked the symbolic dismemberment of the victims to Masonic rituals. One popular theory, discussed by Stephen Knight in his exposé of the Masons, *The Brotherhood*, is that the murders were committed to cover up a major indiscretion committed by a Mason belonging to the highly secretive upper echelons of the most important lodge. There have even been suggestions that this Master Mason could have been a member of the British royal family.

THE ILLUMINATI

Anew world order or world-wide conspiracy is often seen as the stuff of *The X-Files* or similar fictional accounts fueling a paranoid belief in a "Big Brother" government. But before we consign the whole concept to the realm of fantasy, we have to admit that more than once in our history, power-crazed individuals have decided on a political policy of world domination. Wouldn't the whole process be easier if it was not left to one person to steer the world in a certain direction, but a group of secretive and highly influential international figures bonded together using any means they saw possible to advance their plan? That's how the Illuminati allegedly operates—but no one is quite sure who or what is behind it, even the members themselves. The Illuminati may not even exist, but if it does, its aim is thought to be nothing less than world domination.

On May 1, 1776, a Professor of Canon Law at the Bavarian University of Ingolstadt, Adam Weishaupt, formed a group called the Illuminati (meaning "intellectually inspired"). He was a radical thinker who wanted to rid the world of corrupt religion and monarchies, and replace them with his own brand of Gnostic free-thinking. His ideas, based on the popular beliefs of intellectuals of the time, embraced occultism, spirituality, and even alchemy.

Some commentators have alleged that Weishaupt was just a front, and the real power behind the Illuminati came from the Rothschild family. Others have linked his group to the Knights Templar, saying it was simply another guise by which the Templars maintained their power. Whatever the truth, the group quickly attracted some of Germany's most radical minds, including Goethe and Mozart, and within a few years had a network of approximately 2,000 powerful followers. Weishaupt was a clever man, and initiated people who would be of use to his plans. He used any means possible, even resorting to extortion and blackmail to "encourage" powerful people,

such as the Duc D'Orleans, to help further the cause.

It was important for Weishaupt to infiltrate the Freemasons, as a cover for his group's activities, and to swell their number with like-minded individuals. He also instigated a similar tiered system of initiation where devoted followers could climb the ladder of importance, being allowed more intimate knowledge of the group's aims. In reality, only a tiny circle of people knew the organization was working to overthrow first the French monarchy and then the Pope.

*T*he all-seeing eye, the ancient symbol used by those secretly working toward world domination, according to conspiracy theorists.

The Illuminati was making powerful enemies, and although they had woven a web of highly influential members, the established Jesuit Church was determined to quash its power. It pressurized the French government into banning the organization, which is what happened in 1785. The Church helped fuel the suspicions about the society by publishing a variety of anti-Illuminati leaflets and articles. They implied that the group was responsible for most domestic disorder, starting the conspiracy theories which have survived into modern times. A book published in 1993, *Secret Societies and their Power in the 20th Century*, by Jan van Helsing, links the Illuminati to the Second World War, the Russian Revolution, the Kennedy assas-sination, Scientology, and the Gulf War, not to mention the CIA, FBI, and the Vatican!

Although some members were imprisoned in 1785, Weishaupt escaped, and it is thought the group reconvened in France. The upheaval and political climate suited their ideas, and it is thought they worked hard to create disharmony among the French population. Some researchers have suggested the whole French Revolution was orchestrated by the group, perhaps in revenge for the deaths of the Knights Templar at the hands of the French monarchy in 1310.

Jan van Helsing's book suggests that the Bavarian Illuminati were (or perhaps still are) only a very small

Influential thinkers have been attracted to the group's radical philosophy, including financier Baron Lionel Rothschild (above left), philosopher Jean Jacques Rousseau (above), and composer Mozart (left).

THE BILDERBERG GROUP

One organization that has been linked with Weishaupt's Bavarian Illuminati is the secretive Bilderberg Group, which meets once a year. Formed in 1954 by Prince Bernhard of Holland, the group's estimated 120 members are the wealthiest, most powerful and scholarly minds of our time. *The Scotsman* newspaper said critics had described the group as a "shadow world government," and the paper went on to say that the group has even been credited with orchestrating the downfall of British Prime Minister Margaret Thatcher.

Each annual conference is conducted with great secrecy. The delegates, all from Europe and North America, meet and discuss world politics completely off the record. It is thought that the power the delegates command between them, and the influence they have on political parties, is substantial. They are also thought to be behind the setting up of a smaller organization of approximately forty of the most powerful businessmen in Europe, who also meet to discuss how to influence European policy.

The Group claims it is just a forum for discussion, but critics are suspicious of the secrecy of the meetings and the presence of influential figures, such as the Rockefeller family, is bound to worry conspiracy theorists.

25

part of a much bigger plot to enforce a "new world order." He believes that actual power is in the hands of a very small number of extremely wealthy families. In effect, according to the elusive Van Helsing, many monarchies, governments, and even the United Nations are being manipulated from behind the scenes by a complex group of individuals who probably don't even know they are in the pay of the Illuminati. Whether this is just paranoid fantasy, or whether the existence of groups like the Bilderberg Group gives the theory some credence, is up to the individual to decide.

MODERN DRUIDS

*E*nglish Druids celebrating the summer solstice at the ancient
mystical site of Stonehenge, Wiltshire.

Druids followed an ancient form of worship which is shrouded in mystery. Modern Druids, although they appear similarly dressed at official functions, follow practices that aren't that closely related to their secretive forefathers. Most people's image of the modern-day Druids is as a group of peace-loving pagans who gather round Stonehenge in England at the time of the summer solstice, but ancient Druids were a much more bloodthirsty group, presiding over multiple sacrifices, many of the victims being human.

In June 1998, English Heritage, which looks after many of the UK's ancient and historical interest sites, announced it would allow pagans to worship at Stonehenge for the first time in ten years—damage to the ancient stones caused by too many over-enthusiastic revelers meant the organization was cautious about allowing people too near. Whereas once the monument could be approached via fields and people could touch the

giant, cold stones, now the public are kept at a distance by a roped barrier. The monument, with its famous circle of huge stone pillars, visible for miles on the flat land of Salisbury Plain, has often been linked with the Druids, but they didn't build the monument, they only worshiped there. The present Arch Druid of Britain, Rollo Maughfling, told newspapers: "It's our most revered site, holiest of holy sites."

Druidry is thought to have existed for over two thousand years. Although the information is patchy, mainly gleaned from conflicting written accounts by the Romans, it is thought they originated in France some time before 400 BC, and then spread across Celtic Europe. With the growth of Christianity, it seems that not only the role of the Druids was diminished, but they may have been actively persecuted for their pagan beliefs. It wasn't until the early sixteenth century that a revival took place, but by this time many ancient stories and

SACRIFICES TO THE GODS

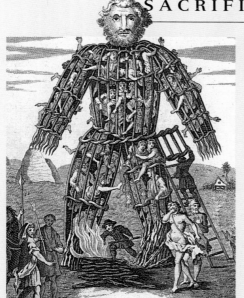

One of the rituals that the modern Druid orders haven't revived is human sacrifice. It seems the Celts were superstitious about many things, and one way to ensure good health or good luck was to offer a live gift to the gods.

Sacrifice was an important tradition, overseen by the Druids. Roman records of the time speak of altars draped with body parts. Some even mention horrible mutilations and cannibalism, but this may well have been exaggeration on the part of the rather biased invaders.

One form of sacrifice, which some historians believe several Celtic tribes practiced and was overseen by the Druids, was that of the Wicker Man. A huge figure was built of sticks, wood, and natural fibers, the "man" was filled with live animals and sometimes humans, and the whole thing was then burnt as an offering to the Gods. Modern Druids sometimes construct Wicker Men as part of their rituals, but they are, of course, burnt without the living sacrifices.

ANCIENT **D**RUIDS PRESIDED OVER SACRIFICES, MANY OF THE VICTIMS HUMAN

traditions, which had always been passed on by word of mouth, had been lost.

Today there are Druid organizations as far afield as Australia and the USA. The Council of British Druids is a central body that oversees the various groups, but there are no hard and fast rules about worship. Most do have a basic set of ideals, though, grounded in a love for nature, a belief in the power of pre-Christian gods and goddesses, and a belief in self-fulfillment as long as it doesn't hurt anyone else.

The ancient Druids weren't technically a cult—they were most probably just a well-respected "layer" or "class" of society consisting not only of priests, but musicians, healers, those interested in legal affairs, and various other professions. The Druids had an all-encompassing attitude to life and its essence. Everything had spirit, and therefore everything was interconnected. When a person died, their soul was simply reincarnated into the otherworld, and then when that body died, they were reincarnated back into the human world. Death wasn't a cause for mourning, but celebrating.

Modern Druids, the largest group of whom call themselves the Order of Bards, Ovates and Druids (OBOD), are more concerned with maintaining the spiritual aspect of Druidry than the more bloodthirsty past. They cherish the long history of the movement, and highlight the importance the Order has always placed on the natural environment. Philip Carr-Gorman, one of the spokespeople for the OBOD, summed up the modern movement's ideology in an interview with writer John Shreeve, saying: "Druidry is still about being on the land and opening up to the elements and to the stars."

Some groups try to maintain what others see as a romanticized version of the ancient Druids' rites and beliefs, but most established groups believe in actively researching the mystical ancient Order, to understand its role in Celtic society better. The Order of Bards, Ovates and Druids tries to keep the spiritual aspect alive, and has recently been involved with the active anti-road protest movement in the UK, campaigning against the destruction of the countryside. At its very simplest level, Druidry embraces a love for the planet and each other, and tries to replace the stresses of modern living with some magic and mysticism.

27

Chapter Two

NEW RELIGIOUS MOVEMENTS

ESOTERIC AND CHRISTIAN OFFSHOOT CULTS

"NEW RELIGIOUS MOVEMENTS" has become the politically correct term for groups which fall within the description of a "cult," but which are seeking a less stigmatized definition of their role within society. The term is also used when the size of membership of a cult means it has the power to try to establish itself as either a religion or a nonprofitmaking institution in the eyes of the law.

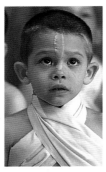

Despite their size, popularity, and considerable wealth, these groups have all been witness to practices that are either illegal or are considered morally questionable to the majority of Western society. This doesn't mean they haven't offered their members something beneficial—indeed, the many thousands of people who belong to these cults have obviously found a way of life that suits them. The groups in this chapter do not necessarily have similarities. Some, such as the International Society for Krishna Consciousness and the Church of Jesus Christ of Latter-Day Saints, are renowned for their charitable works, and it is their history that warrants their inclusion. Others, such as the Unification Church, tend to shroud themselves in secrecy, which has led to massive media campaigns warning of supposed dangers.

The growth in popularity of these groups is probably based in the deep-rooted dissatisfaction that some people feel with their lives nowadays. Returning to a spiritual base, where a simple life can be achieved, is tempting to most of us at some point. Unfortunately, some of these groups end up not rejecting the uglier side of modern life, but embracing its obsession with money, power, and greed. When this happens, they become the exact opposite of what their trusting devotees expected, but by then it is often too late.

The spectacular sight of a Moonie mass wedding. Each bride, dressed identically, holds a picture of her husband-to-be. The wedding day may be the first time the couple have met.

THE CHURCH *of* JESUS CHRIST *of* LATTER-DAY SAINTS

The Church of Jesus Christ of Latter-Day Saints is better known as the Mormon Church, and has approximately 10 million members world-wide. The modern organization has an excellent public image, unsullied by the court cases or rumors of impropriety that beset certain other groups. Indeed, the Church is so well organized in the USA that most would rank it alongside the more mainstream religious groups. This acceptance is based on the clean-living, generous and caring attitude of most Mormons, yet the history of the group is far from mainstream—it has links to Freemasonry and clairvoyance, as well as embracing unChristian beliefs such as polygamy, and blood atonement.

Today, the Mormon Church is flourishing, not only in numbers but in terms of wealth, and the main group has its spectacular headquarters in Salt Lake City, Utah. A breakaway group, the Reorganized Church of Jesus Christ of Latter-Day Saints, considers itself the true Mormon Church, although it has far fewer members—a few hundred thousand rather than millions. There are also many splinter groups, almost exclusively based in the USA, which tend to be more fundamentalist in their beliefs, some still actively practicing polygamy, and the main Church very often denies any links with them.

The movement was started by Joseph Smith in 1830 in New York State. This coincided with the printing of *The Book of Mormon* that Smith had been dictating for the previous three years. When he was 14, he allegedly consulted God about which of the many Churches he should join. God told him to wait and He would show him the true way. Three years later, an angel called Moroni was sent to guide Smith to a nearby hill, and he

Brigham Young, hailed as a Mormon prophet, traveled west with a small group of followers to establish the settlement at Salt Lake City, Utah.

was shown where a series of gold plates depicting the early history of America and the real gospel were buried. Smith was told he would be able to translate the ancient hieroglyphics with a pair of magical "spectacles" that would be found nearby. According to Smith, Moroni was the last of a race of Israelites which had once populated America. His father, Mormon, had documented their race's existence and how Christ had appeared to them on the golden plates, which his son then hid in the ground.

Smith translated the texts to various people, including his wife and best friend, while sitting behind a curtain. Six other people testified to having seen the plates, although they later left the Church and claimed the "seeing" had been more a matter of faith than a physical experience. Smith returned the plates to Moroni when he had finished his translations.

The Book of Mormon caused a stir. Although it is heavily based on the Bible, many of its doctrines are quite far removed. Smith taught that God is a physical being who procreates with his wives (more than one!), producing spirit children. These spirits descend to earth and take up residence in the bodies of human babies. By living the life of a good Mormon, humans can achieve almost "god" status, and will ascend to God's planet and produce spirit children themselves. Mormons taught that God visited earth to beget Jesus with Mary, and that Jesus himself was married—not once, but three times.

The emphasis on the family and having children is central to Mormonism even today, but in its early stages it meant that the Church embraced the practice of polygamy. Today, if asked, the group will say that the practice was adopted to protect the women, of whom there were more than men, and they are quick to point

MULTIPLE MARRIAGES

***R**ight: A poolside baptism of a new member into the Church.*

***B**elow: The 150th anniversary of the 1,000 mile trek to Utah is relived by Mormon families dressed in authentic costume and riding in wagons.*

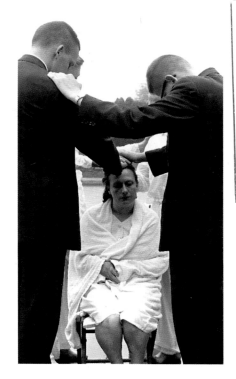

31

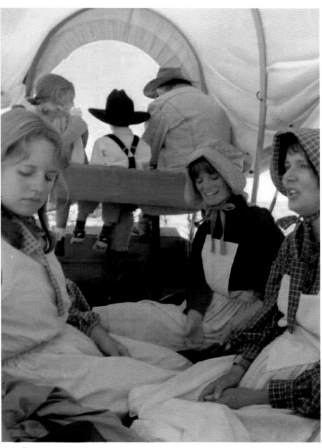

Although the main Mormon Church outlawed polygamy in 1890, various splinter groups still practice it today. According to Britain's Channel 4 *Witness* program, "The Polygamists," there are an estimated 30,000 people involved in polygamous relationships in the Utah area, most of whom look to Joseph Smith and Brigham Young's teachings. Brigham Young declared: "The only men who become gods are those who enter into polygamy."

Polygamous families are said to be ideal, as they produce many children (contraception is frowned upon). In reality, they seem to be hard work for the women involved, who must rein in personal feelings and live with the knowledge their husband is having a sexual relationship with at least one other woman. Men usually visit their wives on a roster basis, and they often stay at home, preferring to spend their time preaching while the women work and finance the family.

Children are expected to marry within the small communities as well, and it is not unusual for what most people would consider very strange arrangements to take place, such as two sisters marrying the same man. These fundamentalist groups believe they are following the true Mormon teachings, although most mainstream Church members now totally denounce the practice. Although polygamy is still illegal in the USA, and has been since 1890, the authorities haven't shown much active interest since the 1950s, when some families were arrested and had their children taken into state care.

JOSEPH SMITH

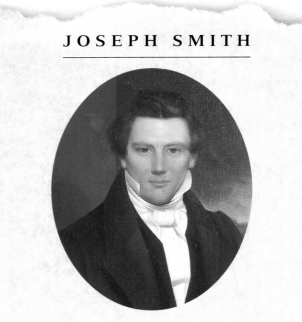

The founder of the Church of Jesus Christ of Latter-Day Saints has been the subject of some controversy. Joseph Smith was born in Sharon, Vermont, in 1805. Smith's mother, Lucy, dabbled in white witchcraft, telling fortunes and having "visions." His father was supposed to have had a fondness for alcohol as well as being obsessed with digging for treasure. The family apparently wasn't well thought of by their neighbors, and more than one commentator has suggested that the young Smith wasn't known for his truthfulness. Despite this rather inauspicious start, Smith became the figurehead of a massive, well-respected and very rich institution. He was murdered in 1844, and left behind at least twenty wives.

out that it was officially declared an excommunicable offence in 1890. Polygamy was only practiced by men. Women were actually seen as inferior, only ascending to be with God if they had married a good husband.

Joseph Smith settled with his 20,000 followers in Nauvoo, Illinois, in 1838, but his subsequent demands for members to be polygamous, and a series of internal disputes with other leaders led to him being imprisoned for trying to subdue his critics with force. While he was being held with his brother Hyrum in jail in 1844, the building was raided by angry Church of Jesus Christ of Latter-Day Saints members, who shot the two men dead.

Brigham Young, a zealous young Mormon missionary who had already attracted about 7,000 converts from his

YOUNG BELIEVED THAT SOMETIMES IT MIGHT BE NECESSARY TO KILL A SINNER TO SAVE HIS SOUL

two-year stay in the UK, took over after alleging that Smith had named him as his successor, but after two years of continuous squabbles, the group split. Some members stayed with Smith's first wife, waiting until his son (also called Joseph Smith) could take over as the rightful heir. They went on to form a new group called the Reorganized Church of Jesus Christ of Latter-Day Saints, which is still based in Nauvoo. They quickly rejected some of Smith's more radical beliefs.

Brigham Young believed firmly in polygamy and blood atonement (the belief that Jesus's bloodshed was not enough to atone for all our sins, and sometimes it might be necessary to kill a sinner in order to save his soul). He took a small group of less than two hundred on a trek that modern Mormons compare to that of Moses. After months of traveling through the

Left: The dramatic spires of the opulent Mormon Temple in Salt Lake City.

desert, Young decided that he would establish his new city on the shores of Great Salt Lake in Utah. Thousands followed the initial pilgrims, irrigated the desert soil and built one of the finest, cleanest, and safest cities in the USA. Today, the glorious white Temple stands resplendent as testament to the work of those initial inhabitants, and it is seen as the headquarters of the whole international movement.

This new homeland wasn't without controversy, though. Brigham Young is heralded as a prophet, and therefore in direct communication with God, but his obsession with blood atonement isn't widely publicized. He was responsible for ordering the deaths of 120 people who were traveling across the group's land. He also had 25 wives.

Today, the Church is nowhere near as fundamentalist, and it works hard within the community, often running charitable groups, but it has maintained some of its former practices. Devout Mormons wear a long undergarment beneath their clothes, which is thought to bring them closer to God. Young men in the organization still consider it an honor to serve as a missionary for two years. They are often sent to different countries and spend up to twelve hours a day knocking on doors and talking to people about the group. They work hard, and have to record all their daily news in a diary that is sent back to their own church. Members also donate 10 percent of their earnings to the organization, they don't indulge in pre- or extramarital sex, they abstain from drugs, alcohol, tea, and coffee, and don't believe in using contraception.

One of the only mysteries about the group that survives today is the Temple itself. Not all Mormons go to their Temple—most simply attend their local churches. Some of the more unusual practices are baptizing people who are already dead, and sealing marriages for eternity. The former takes place on a regular basis, although it is apparently expensive. It is important to baptize dead relatives who weren't Mormons so they too can ascend to be with God. Mormons are notorious for researching their family trees to discover relatives who need this service. Marriages are also bonded at the Temple, because it is believed you can maintain the same partner after death, and therefore

THE OSMONDS

The most famous members of the Mormon organization are the seven members of the 1960s group the Osmonds. The family follows all the Mormon traditional moral values, and their success was due in part to this welcome change from the excesses of the era. Their parents, who fans refer to as "Mom and Dad," went through a marriage for eternity in the Salt Lake City Temple. They had nine children, seven of whom formed the Osmonds pop group, which went on to have 34 gold and platinum records. The two eldest sons are hearing-impaired, and according to the family's official literature, were "the first deaf missionaries sent out by the Church of Jesus Christ of Latter-Day Saints." They served their two years spreading the word in Canada. The family has its own charitable organization, the Osmond Foundation, which raises money for children.

33

produce spirit children with your spouse in the afterlife.

Privileged members are not supposed to reveal what takes place in the Temple, although it is thought the ceremonies have many links with Masonic rituals, including the symbolism and the male superiority. In an effort to become more open, the group does allow outsiders to look around their temples, but only before they are due to be opened. In Preston, England, on Sunday June 7, 1998, the Church of Jesus Christ of Latter-Day Saints opened their second largest temple in the world. Around 100,000 people visited the magnificent building, which allegedly cost between $75 million and $150 million to build, before it shut its doors to nonmembers for good.

THE UNIFICATION CHURCH

*T*he mass wedding of 30,000 Moonie couples at the Olympic Stadium, Seoul, in 1992,
presided over by Reverend and Mrs Moon, center stage.

The multi-million-dollar organization popularly known as the "Moonies" is really a business empire that encompasses private property, over eighty types of business including newspapers, and a well-established Church of totally loyal members who donate all their wealth to the cause. It is an empire that is not only growing, with an estimated 3 million members, but has also been linked to some of the worst allegations of brainwashing. The group famously settled out of court in 1989 when two American ex-members, David Molko and Tracey Leal, filed for compensation on the grounds they had been falsely imprisoned and had suffered emotional distress.

The most public face of the Moonies was the 1992 spectacle of 30,000 brides and grooms getting married in one mass ceremony in the Olympic Stadium in Seoul, South Korea. All were dressed identically, and all gave their partners identical rings. It was the biggest mass wedding ever to take place. All the participants had had their partners chosen for them by the Moonies' leader, the Reverend Sung Myung Moon, and some had never met before the ceremony, having only seen each other in photographs. Nearly all of them were young, in their twenties, and well-educated.

Young people seem to be particularly susceptible to the Moonies' recruiting tactics. Some parents have had to have their children kidnapped and then "deprogramed" after they ran away to join the cult. Steve Hassan, author of *Combatting Cult Mind Control: Protection, Rescue and Recovery from Destructive Cults*, says: "I have no qualms about referring to the Unification Church as a destructive cult." He should know, because he himself was recruited into the organization when he was at college, and now he works as an expert helping other former members return to normal society.

Hassan recounts how he was a disillusioned student, recently split up from a girlfriend and desperate to find his way in life, when he was approached by a group of people calling themselves the One World Crusade. It was only much later that he realized the group actually

MOONIES ARE NOTORIOUS FOR THEIR DEVIOUS METHODS OF RAISING CHURCH FUNDS

belonged to the Moonies.

Hassan and other critics have said that Moon is keen to recruit young people because they will work hard for him. They certainly have to. Although Moon is an excellent businessman and has invested wisely, the Church's great wealth has been built up by the devoted labors of members. Once they have joined, Moonies are told they must make money for the organization. They are notorious for their devious methods of raising funds on the streets, going door to door with pictures, plants, and bric-à-brac. They won't disclose where the money is going, and will lie if asked (Moon says this is fine). Moonies don't recruit while they are selling—they are just expected to reach or beat the target they've been given, even if it means collecting cash from unsuspecting barroom drinkers late at night.

Using classic cult tactics, members are expected to live in a commune, give up their possessions, cut ties with family members, and make no decisions for themselves. It is this total lack of responsibility that is so attractive to some young people, and it isn't unusual for members to have joined because the outside world was overwhelming, or they thought they were underachieving. At the recruitment sessions, they will have found a group of friendly, like-minded people who make them feel part of a safe family network. They are also promised they will be saved from Satan.

When the Unification Church started to recruit in the UK during the 1970s and 1980s, the media launched a massive publicity campaign against its tactics. The Church tried to sue the *Daily Mail* newspaper for libel, but lost and had to make a record payment (at that time). Despite an active PR campaign, the group has never really gained a hold in the UK. It is much more successful in Japan and the USA, and has been busy recruiting in the former Soviet Union, France, China, and various South American countries. Moon's ultimate plan is that his Church will become a political force and take over the world, destroying communism.

The Church was officially started in 1954, but it was when he was 16 that Sung Myung Moon had a revelation from God. He was told he was the third Adam, and that his mission was to complete the message Christ brought

35

REV. AND MRS MOON

Although Moon instructs his followers that marriage is sacred, and even ensures their unions are blessed by choosing their partners for them, Mrs Moon is either his third or fourth wife (reports vary as to whether he ever married his third). Members justify this by saying it took a long time to find the right Heavenly Mother. Hak Ja Han, whom he married in 1960 and who has borne him 12 children, apparently fulfills the requirements set down by God.

Moon's first wife divorced him after he was imprisoned in his homeland of Korea in 1945. The official reason is that his views were considered extremist, although some commentators have suggested he was linked with either bigamy or adultery, but the facts are very sketchy on this point.

Far removed from any scandal of that nature, the Moon family now lives on a 22-acre estate in New York State. Contact with their group's members is rare, although Rev. and Mrs Moon do still officiate at the mass weddings, when they appear decked out in white and gold robes, with crowns on their heads.

to earth, but which was aborted because he was crucified. Moon tries not to call himself the Second Messiah, but in effect that is how his disciples see him.

According to Moon, Adam was supposed to father a perfect human family, but Eve was seduced by Lucifer (the serpent) and the resulting child was tainted. Jesus

Below: American Unification Church supporters protest outside the court at Moon's trial for tax evasion in New York City, 1981.

36

was then apparently sent to try again, but before he found the perfect woman to procreate with, he was killed. Moon is, according to his own teachings, charged by God with finishing Jesus's teachings and creating the perfect family. He was chosen after God had spent the last 2,000 years looking for someone, because he has led a perfect, sinless life and has devoted himself to the true God. Only those who are procreated by him, or those entering into marriages blessed by him, are deemed to be free of sin and worthy of salvation.

He has published a book on his theology entitled *Divine Principle*, which is read in conjunction with the Bible, but is thought to be superior because it contains "updates" from God. Moon is not only in contact with God, but has claimed he can "talk to" the great prophets, such as Jesus and Buddha. Not all God's plans are revealed in the book. Moon has implied he knows a lot more about our planet's future, which he will reveal when God is ready. One of

the Moonies' recruiting tactics is to tell those having doubts that everyone will join the Unification Church one day—so they might as well join now.

Recruiting is carried out with as little regard to truth as is collecting funds. Their "heavenly deception" stretches to befriending people who seemed likely to join, and then inviting them for weekends away without once mentioning their association with the Moonies. Surrounded by so-called friends, the new recruits are taken to a commune where they participate in games and a few soul-searching seminars. Most of the recruits will not be new at all, but according to ex-members are already converts who pretend to be at ease about revealing their darkest secrets and denouncing their parents. The process, dubbed "love-bombing," would wear down even the most doubtful person eventually.

Ideally, a new recruit spends a couple of weeks adjusting to commune life. During that period they aren't allowed any time to themselves, they must absorb Moon's teachings (but not all of them in this first intense session), they must recognize Rev. and Mrs Moon as their true family, and experience the importance of raising funds for the organization. They will have had very little sleep, but will undoubtedly feel elated after being accepted into a huge family where members are told to always smile.

Everything is decided for members in the commune, which makes life very regimented, but also in a sense very easy. The sexes are kept apart, and a clean-living approach is adopted—no drugs, tobacco, alcohol, or extravagances are allowed. All meals and essentials are provided, and even if the surroundings are far from luxurious, there isn't generally time to dwell on it.

Moon's doctrines are closely tied to his political beliefs, so he sees no reason why he should stay out of political life. He has aspirations to eventually put some of his followers in the White House, and it is already well known that he has had dealings with major politicians. He has an intense hatred of communism, no doubt because of his problems back in Korea, so much so that his views have often taken the other extreme. He allegedly gave monetary backing to Jean-Marie Le Pen's rightwing campaigns in France, and has tried to befriend major politicians in the US government. He only approached Russia with a view to gaining new converts once communism was truly dead and buried.

Ex-members have led the campaign against the cult. They were delighted when Moon was convicted of fraud

MOON HAS IMPLIED HE KNOWS A LOT MORE ABOUT OUR PLANET'S FUTURE

in 1982. He hadn't paid taxes on some personal funds, claiming it was Church money and therefore exempt. He was fined and spent over a year in jail. Although many ex-Moonies donated a substantial sum of money when they joined, most see their time in the cult as a period of servitude, and some have also tried to sue for the equivalent of lost earnings. All the money they earned by selling candles and plants, and so on was handed over to the organization, while they worked from early morning to past midnight, often being made to feel guilty when they were so tired they couldn't work any more.

Adjusting to life outside the cult can't be easy either, after being alienated from family and friends, and told that sexual relationships outside marriage are the product of Satan, not to mention never having to think for themselves. So the decision to leave the cult is not always an easy one.

MODERN MOONIE MARRIAGES

Although the group is anxious to clean up its public image, one of the most talked about practices, that of Rev. Moon choosing the partners for marriageable people, still continues. It is seen as the ultimate act of faith by Moonies to trust Moon's judgment in this matter. Devotees have to be celibate for seven years before they are eligible for marriage. They do get a chance to refuse the partner Moon chooses for them, but apparently few do. The engagement between couples is often long as well, culminating in a mass wedding ceremony overseen by Rev. and Mrs Moon.

Couples of different nationality are often joined in marriage, and the emphasis is placed on the sanctity of the bond between the two, rather than "love." Marriage is essentially to form a family of children without sin, so members work hard at making a marriage work, despite the fact they may never have met their partner before the ceremony.

BHAGWAN SHREE RAJNEESH

In 1974, a philosophy student in Poona, India, formed the ultimate cult based on sex. Rajneesh Chandra Mohan renamed himself the Bhagwan Shree Rajneesh ("the blessed one who has recognized himself as God") and set up a commune which had about 6,000 permanent residents, all of whom looked to the balding, long-bearded guru for their lead in life.

His "freedom to do what you want" philosophy attracted many educated Westerners to the group, most of whom parted with large sums of money to help establish their leader's idea of a Utopian city. The Rajneesh was a clever man, an intellectual who had studied religious philosophy and was renowned for being a convincing orator. When he died, he left behind hundreds of books and recordings of his beliefs so the cult could carry on.

His own sexual preferences, a liking for pretty young women, were central to the cult's lifestyle, which promoted a total lack of inhibitions. Like most cults with links to Eastern traditions, the Rajneesh utilized the emphasis on "self" to encourage his followers to reject the constraints of their past and adopt a free-love philosophy. In reality, the Rajneesh was "brainwashing" his followers by forcing them to work long hours and then take part in disorientating meditation sessions which would often result in a free-for-all orgy.

Members of the Poona-based society wore orange or red robes, a pendant with the Rajneesh's

THE MASTER OF FREE LOVE

Born Chandra Mohan, but nicknamed Rajneesh "the king" by his family, he was the eldest of 13 children, and was brought up by his grandparents in India. Although they weren't wealthy, he was given a good education. He was an unruly pupil, often arguing with his teachers and apparently leading his fellow classmates astray, but all accounts of his childhood report him as being very intelligent. After gaining a degree in philosophy, he taught the subject for ten years, and by the time he set up his commune, he was quite well regarded as a freethinker and lecturer. He gave himself the title of "bhagwan," which he said meant "the blessed one."

Members say he had a good sense of humor and liked nothing better than to have a good argument, although it does seem he was addicted to Valium and other drugs. Some reports mention bouts of severe depression when the guru would withdraw from his followers and allow a team of top-ranking women to run the group. He died in 1990, aged 59. He always maintained he had been poisoned while in US custody, although some writers have suggested he may well have been poisoned—but by someone from within the cult. Others have implied the guru died from an Aids-related illness.

image on it, and if you were female, a lack of underwear was desirable. They were checked for cleanliness, especially their hair, which had to be washed thoroughly, and hands had to be cleaned in pure alcohol. He called his followers "sannyasins," after the Hindu word "sannyas" meaning "holy people."

Followers tended to be wealthy—indeed, the guru preached that poor people couldn't reach full enlightenment because they were too concerned with material things. This was convenient, as the cult demanded a constant flow of money into its accounts. Writer Jean Ritchie reports that some people resorted to prostitution or smuggling drugs from the East back to the West to finance their stay in the Rajneesh's Utopia.

By convincing his followers that concepts such as truth, guilt, and sin were man-made hindrances that could be washed away by deep meditation, he was in fact ridding the sannyasins of their grip on reality. They operated totally within the guru's rules, and as the movement progressed, would undertake serious life-altering decisions based purely on what he believed was right.

Meditation sessions went on for hours on end. Often conducted while followers were naked, they would be instructed to perform bizarre techniques such as spinning round and round until they could no longer stand. They were told these methods were to clear the head of all

Right: The sannyasins enjoyed group meditation sessions overseen personally by the Bhagwan.

Below: The Bhagwan famously toured his American commune in one of his many Rolls-Royce cars.

TRUTH, GUILT, AND SIN COULD BE WASHED AWAY BY DEEP MEDITATION

but that this was apparently condoned by the Rajneesh.

Although there were many teachers running recruiting groups all over the world, back at Poona, the Rajneesh favored personally overseeing the meditation sessions. He taught that through sexual intercourse a person achieved the nearest possible feeling of letting go of all their inhibitions and therefore experiencing true spirituality. He claimed that by experimenting sexually, and as often as possible, one would eventually be able to reach this ecstatic state without sex, and therefore people would become celibate. He later added to this theory, saying that when this happened, a perfect race of spiritual beings could be genetically engineered, instead of the weak children that the claustrophobic and defunct family unit was currently producing.

Although this teaching was based on Tantric sex, and

thoughts and put them in direct touch with their inner spirituality. Meditation sessions often took place in padded rooms to stop people hurting themselves when they fell.

Nevertheless, ex-members have said that there were many injuries at these sessions because their guru often demanded they let go of any anger they were feeling. This resulted in other members being beaten and kicked as frustrations were raised to a frenzy. There are also reports that in some of these sessions women were raped,

*T*he commune at Poona after the death of the Bhagwan. Followers still gather
to learn from his teachings.

many of the group's publicity shots show couples practicing massage and other acts together, in reality the meditation sessions often encouraged people to swap partners, or join in group orgies. People who found it difficult to be so "enlightened" were sneered at. The Rajneesh took many of the young girls to his own bed, once famously claiming he had had sex with more women than any other man on earth, although it seems he enjoyed watching proceedings more than taking part himself. The women tended to see it as the ultimate accolade to be chosen by their master.

Local people were horrified at this influx of amoral people who had parties on the beaches that usually ended with outdoor orgies. Allegations of drug use and smuggling started circulating, as did reports of the rapes and beatings. When the Indian government started investigating the cult's tax payments, or rather lack of them, the Rajneesh quickly moved to the USA.

Famously arriving in the USA with 12 tons of luggage, the Rajneesh purchased a huge area of land in Antelope, Oregon, for an impressive $1.5 million in cash! Over the next few years, millions of dollars were spent on building Utopia. The Rajneesh lived in splendor, his impressive quarters being completed first, and he drove around the commune in one of his much-favored Rolls-Royce cars (he was alleged to have owned 93 of them). Followers lived in squalor. The commune had been called "Rajneeshpuram" by the guru, but most referred to it as "Big Muddy Ranch," its apt original name.

While the guru had married a US citizen to be allowed entry into the country, most of the followers were there illegally on traveler's permits. They were also illegally claiming as much state help as possible. Things changed for the followers when they arrived in the USA, but because they were so used to following the guru's wishes, 4,000 people stayed on. Signs of paranoia among the

HE ONCE
FAMOUSLY
CLAIMED TO
HAVE HAD
SEX WITH
MORE
WOMEN
THAN ANY
OTHER MAN

highest ranks were showing. The Rajneesh was followed everywhere by an armed bodyguard of trained men, some from a privately hired security firm. Most phones in the commune were tapped to establish which followers weren't completely loyal to the guru, and members were forbidden to leave unless a real emergency happened.

When the Rajneesh went into one of his reclusive periods, which he did more and more often, a circle of women led by his personal assistant, Ma Anand Sheela, took over the day-to-day running of affairs. Sheela was obsessed with increasing the group's fundraising, and pressurized members to donate more generously. Those who couldn't afford to stay on were asked to leave.

Rajneesh's plans for his empire got out of control. He built on his own land without seeking planning permission, and then tried to take over the town of Antelope, where he gained control of the local government and started renaming all the streets. A team of followers contaminated local restaurants with home-grown salmonella virus, and critics of the commune were heavily intimidated.

After the group shipped in thousands of homeless people from around the country to try to swell the numbers of sympathetic followers, the state of Oregon had had enough.

At the ranch, it seems that the paranoia had reached an all-time high. Ma Anand Sheela, who was in effect in control of the cult at this stage, disappeared to Germany, where she was later arrested and extradited back to the USA. A month later, the Rajneesh was arrested. Newspaper reports showed the guru in a long, striped robe, being led away in handcuffs.

Sheela was sentenced to 20 years' imprisonment for her part in various frauds, phone tapping, orchestrating the salmonella incident (over 700 of the town's population were ill as a result), drug smuggling, and arson. It was alleged at the trial that she was the power behind the cult, and that the attempts to take over Antelope by sabotaging elections were all her idea. Her sentence was later reduced to four years.

The Rajneesh himself got off more lightly. He was

MURDER PLOT FOILED

In 1995, Sally Anne Croft and Susan Hagan faced a US judge on charges of conspiring to murder lawyer Charles Turner. Both women had been members of the Rajneesh cult and had helped plan a murder, which never took place, of a lawyer who was threatening to expose the cult's more dubious activities. The women, who were extradited from the UK despite pleas from senior politicians, were found guilty of the crime they had committed ten years earlier.

Judge Malcolm Marsh gave the two women what he considered were lenient sentences of five years each because he had received so many character witness reports and because he realized they had been under the influence of a cult. Turner had been investigating allegations of multiple fraud.

charged with offences relating to immigration laws, and was ordered to leave the USA. He eventually settled back in Poona, after trying to enter various countries, including the UK and Ireland. A few loyal cult members followed him, and a few stayed on at Big Muddy, but the majority dispersed. The cult still exists—it is mostly based at the former Poona site—although it is now involved with holding meditation conferences all over the world, and has its own Internet presence. The head of the cult is a Canadian known as Swami Prem Jayesh. The cult, which now calls itself Osho International, claims 10,000 believers travel to their commune every year to celebrate what they call "Buddhafield."

TRANSCENDENTAL MEDITATION

Transcendental Meditation (TM) became famous in the 1960s when George Harrison took the other members of the Beatles to meet a little-known guru with long straggly hair. At the time, Maharishi Mahesh Yogi had set up a small study group in Wales, but as soon as the press discovered he was being visited by the world's most famous pop group, everyone wanted to know about his teachings.

The techniques involved have been taught world-wide and were widely acclaimed in the early 1970s, even being taught in schools across the USA. Today, after lengthy US court cases, TM has been officially declared a religion, which means institutions cannot teach it. However, their own literature states: "You don't have to change your lifestyle or beliefs. It is not a religion or a philosophy. It is a practical technique practiced by millions of people world-wide which leads to a fuller, richer and more rewarding life."

At the height of its popularity, the Maharishi promised practitioners would achieve personal satisfaction as well as being able to change the world. If enough followers meditated at the same time, then international crime rates would fall, wars would end, and even stock market prices would rise. He also promised they would fly—but more of that later.

The Maharishi bases his principles on those of Hinduism: that God is everywhere, even within ourselves, and all we have to do to reach Him is "tune into" our inner consciousness. This "fourth state" is the one that most practitioners find when they use the Maharishi's form of meditation, and it is said to lead to improved health, a more creative outlook on life, and inner happiness. There are three higher levels that can be achieved beyond this fourth state, and it is apparently TM's goal to bring the entire world to the point where there is no sin and everyone has attained a level of pure consciousness.

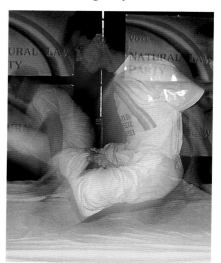

*M*embers of the Natural Law Party demonstrate yogic flying to promote TM as part of their political campaign in Britain.

New members attend a ceremony where a teacher evokes the presence of the Maharishi's own inspiration, Guru Dev, a religious teacher who told the Maharishi to develop a form of meditation for everyone in the world. At the end of the ceremony, they are given their own personal mantra, which they must never reveal to anyone. This mantra must be chanted for 20 minutes in the morning and 20 minutes in the afternoon. All other thoughts should be left to float from the mind as the TM practitioner sits cross-legged on the floor and totally absorbs themself in the meditation. In theory, all stress, illness and any feelings of guilt will be dissolved. Some critics have alleged that the mantras whispered to initiates aren't really 6,000 years old and personalized, but that there are only about 16 in total, which are assigned according to the practitioner's age.

Although the Beatles, Mia Farrow, the Rolling Stones, and the Beach Boys all became famously linked with the supposedly clean-living group, it wasn't long before the fad was over, particularly for the Beatles. After having each donated a week's wages, as all new initiates do, John Lennon famously declared he had had enough and accused the guru of womanizing. With the desertion of his most famous followers, the Maharishi left the UK, declaring: "I know I have failed. My mission is over."

Instead of retiring, as he initially declared he would, the guru successfully reinvented his organization. From his headquarters in Switzerland, the Maharishi initiated his plan to set up 350 TM universities around the world. When there was one TM teacher per thousand people, he said, there would be world peace. In 1976, he introduced a new series of meditation techniques known as the Siddhi Program. Whereas his TM teachings were once again gaining quite a widespread audience, especially in the USA, this new program was for the select few only.

Siddhi, which involved a much more intense form of

RELIGIOUS TRAINING

The Maharishi Mahesh Yogi was born in 1911 in Jabalpur, India. His real name is Mahesh Prasad. When he was 31, he graduated from Allahabad University with a degree in physics. He became interested in yogic meditation while working in a factory, and then allegedly became a Hindu monk. He studied with Guru Dev (also known as Swami Krishanand Saraswati) in the Himalayas for 13 years before his master died, leaving him instructions to set up a universal meditation program.

Pictures of the Maharishi famously show him with long, often unkempt hair, a long robe, sandals, and carrying or wearing flowers.

Right: The Maharishi with the Beatles, his most famous followers.

Below: Spiritual exercises are the key to TM. Meditation is practiced at least once a day.

43

meditation—and incidentally, a much larger donation to the cause—promised the world. Special rooms with padded floors are prepared in TM's many schools, and there, cross-legged and in a meditative state, practitioners can learn to fly. They also, allegedly, can levitate, walk through walls and even become invisible. There are photographs, issued by the movement, of this "yogic flying," but it has to be said they do resemble cross-legged people who have either developed the ability to bounce or are aided by a trampoline which is just out of shot. Perhaps that is doing the group a disservice, but in the absence of any definite evidence, one must maintain an open mind. Bob Larson, in his book *Larson's New Book of*

Cults, says two TM organizations in the USA had to pay an ex-member substantial damages in 1987 when he filed a suit against them claiming TM didn't reduce stress or improve his memory, let alone teach him to fly.

Transcendental Meditation's most recent incarnation has been the formation of the political party known as the Natural Law Party. Started in 1992, it funded candidates for 310 parliamentary seats in the British general election on a policy based on the teachings of the Maharishi. Its literature even promoted the technique of yogic flying. Since the high profile campaign, the group has spread its ambitions internationally and regularly sponsors candidates in elections, and lobbies politicians.

THE INTERNATIONAL SOCIETY *for* KRISHNA CONSCIOUSNESS

44

Researcher Jean Ritchie has written of the International Society for Krishna Consciousness (ISKCON): "What started as a peace-loving crusade to bring the Western world nearer to God degenerated into the most vicious and venal of all the cults." It is certainly true that the movement we commonly know as "Hare Krishna" has had a troubled history, which its present members would rather forget.

The organization is now very image-conscious—it has dropped many of its old fundraising methods and is eager to be adopted into mainstream society. It has been praised in the USA and UK for helping drug addicts and the homeless, and the sight of orange-robed, shaven-headed followers is no longer one to be as wary of. However, the group still operates a very strict routine for full-time members, which might be described as "destructive" by cultwatching organizations.

The typical day for a full ISKCON member starts at 3 a.m. with prayers. There is a service for the whole community at 4 a.m., followed by individual chanting until 6 a.m. A scripture study class takes place from 6 a.m. until 7 a.m., where the sacred text *The Bhagavad Gita* is read, absorbed, and explained. Breakfast takes place at 7:30 a.m., and is followed by general communal chores until 10 a.m. From 10 a.m. until 6 p.m., devotees are usually expected to sell books, spread the Hare Krishna message on the streets and help those in need, usually by offering free food. After a meal at 6 p.m., there will be more study and further services, and any remaining chores will be done before bedtime at 10 p.m. It is a long and intense day.

The morning chants take two hours because it takes that long for a follower to say the compulsory japa, the Hare Krishna mantra ("Hare Krishna, Hare Krishna,

Krishna devotees observe a fire ritual. Food such as ghee and grains are thrown into the fire as a sacrifice to the god Krishna. Vegan food is an important part of all worship and is often referred to as "prasadam" which means spiritualized food or food that has been offered to Krishna.

LIFE IN A TEMPLE

The routine for Hare Krishna members who choose to live in one of their temples is hard to adjust to. There is very little time for personal reflection, if any at all, because the idea is to devote all your thoughts to Krishna. The most important part of Hare Krishna life is the cleaning and feeding of the many statues of Hindu idols that reside on an elaborate altar. The statues are said to house Krishna's spirit, and they must be "fed." The food that is offered to them is later eaten by the temple's inhabitants as a way of absorbing part of Krishna.

Krishna, Krishna, Hare Hare, Hare Rama, Hare Rama, Rama, Rama") the required 1,728 times. All the statues in the temple must also be fed and cleansed.

Not all members of the movement live in a group setting, and those who remain outside are generally less strict about their daily routine. For those who do live in temples—and David V. Barrett, in his book *Sects, Cults and Alternative Religions*, suggests there are only about 300 in the UK at the moment—it is not just the routine that is hard. They are expected to give up all meat and fish, and any stimulants (from drugs and alcohol to coffee). Sex is only allowed for the purpose of procreation and is therefore confined to once or twice a month. The sexes also have to sleep apart, and any sign of affection is frowned upon. Women have a particularly tough time, as they have been traditionally seen by the organization as

HARE KRISHNA HAS HAD A TROUBLED PAST WHICH MEMBERS WOULD RATHER FORGET

being objects of temptation and leading the men astray. Male members who reach the highest level of study are said to have achieved the Sannyasa stage. They pledge to be celibate and live their life in poverty.

The Hare Krishna movement was started in America in 1965 by A.C. Shaktivedanta Swami Prabhupada. He had been told by his guru in India to spread the word to the West, so he made the voyage on a ship, and famously arrived in the USA with $8 in his pocket. His teachings were based on the ancient text *The Bhagavad Gita*, which emphasizes that Krishna is the most important of the Hindu gods. Krishna is ever-present in everything and everybody. He created life, and also looks after it. Devotees believe that the body is a hindrance, and the ideal is to be just a spiritual soul. They also believe in reincarnation and karma, so they work to become as spiritually pure as possible, and that way allow Krishna into their hearts. The chanting of the Hare Krishna mantra not only clears the mind of all other trivial thoughts, but frees the soul from the encumbrance of the body. They also believe that actions carried out in the name of Krishna must be good.

Prabhupada's teachings grew in popularity in the liberal area of Greenwich Village in New York City. The mood was ripe for an alternative lifestyle, and many young people were already experimenting with Eastern beliefs. It was a time when young people were being exposed to drugs, and the excesses of the 1960s were beginning to take their toll. To be offered a path to spirituality which put some order back into their lives was appealing. he quickly gained a following among both dropouts and the intellectual community. Prabhupada was particularly successful at convincing people to give up drugs.

The movement spread to the UK, where Beatle

45

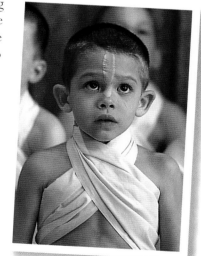

George Harrison publicized the Hare Krishna mantra by recording it as a single which immediately went into the music charts. People became used to seeing the shaven-headed followers chanting and selling their books on streets in most major cities. They gained a reputation for being quite aggressive salespeople. Harrison sold his Hertfordshire mansion to the movement for a very low sum. ISKCON still use the house as their UK headquarters, and it attracts thousands of devotees when they host festivals in its grounds.

ISKCON's mentor died in 1977, which is when problems really started for the group. As an organization, ISKCON was generating large amounts of money throughout its 300 centers world-wide. While Prabhupada was alive, he saw that the money was mostly channeled back into the group's work, and if anyone did stray off the path, he dealt with it. He left instructions just before he died that a council of Sannyasas be formed.

THE MOVEMENT HAS RETURNED TO ITS SPIRITUAL BASE

Accounts vary whether he named any followers he thought should belong to this council, or even if he specified how many council members there should be, but in the end 11 of the most powerful temple leaders claimed responsibility for the movement. They divided up their particular areas of responsibility on a geographical basis, which effectively gave them their own little empires of loyal followers, and they were answerable to no one, apart from Krishna himself.

The years following the guru's death illustrate just how a group which had been criticized only for its proactive selling activities can spiral out of control when greed and paranoia take over. Between 1982 and 1987, the organization was linked to murders, drug dealing, suicide, blackmail, and sexual misdemeanors. In fact, it was more than linked to them—6 out of the 11 so-called spiritual leaders had to leave the organization, bringing some of the worst publicity imaginable.

Today, ISKCON is honest about its troubled past, but emphasizes that the Hare Krishna movement of the 1990s has returned to the spiritual base that A.C. Shaktivedanta Swami Prabhupada so successfully started in 1965. They blame inexperienced leaders, whose background as dropouts from mainstream society and exposure to large amounts of money corrupted their thinking.

One of the first leaders to cause major problems for the society was one of Prabhupada's first US converts. Keith Ham (Kirtananda is his Krishna name) set up a temple in West Virginia, which he called the New Vrindavan. He built a lavish Palace of Gold surrounded by the homes of his flock of Krishna devotees. Several murders are alleged to have taken place at the site, including that of a Krishna devotee who had decided to expose the corruption within New Vrindavan. The stockpiling of weapons was encouraged, and Kirtananda himself was charged with fraud. ISKCON expelled him.

Other leaders, despite the strict vows of celibacy they had taken, had affairs with followers. James Immel (Jayatirtha), head of the English branches, took LSD, and had been having sex with numerous women devotees. Then he was murdered by one of his congregation in 1987. Unnamed leaders are also thought to have indulged in homosexual sex, which, considering the group's stance

FOOD FOR LIFE

In recent years, ISKCON has redeemed itself in the eyes of the media by initiating a well-planned nonprofitmaking organization called Food For Life. In times of international crisis, such as the war in Sarajevo, ISKCON has mobilized neutral food relief teams and managed to penetrate the very areas that need help most. They have received praise from both the Russian and Chechnyan authorities for their relief work, and have played a major part in recent flooding and earthquake disaster relief around the globe. Their feeding centers for the homeless and very poor in inner-city areas of the USA and Australia have also been praised for their nonjudgmental approach to aid.

on sex as a "for procreation only" exercise, was a huge error. Others reportedly asked their followers to steal, sell drugs, use extortion, and blackmail to obtain funds and help them maintain power. The whole situation was one of embarrassment for ISKCON, which cooperated fully with the police over all matters of illegality.

With 6 of the 11 leaders having either left or been expelled, the organization had a radical rethink and abolished the system where a guru had particular control over a certain area. These days, there are more than fifty gurus world-wide, and all are directly answerable to the ISKCON organization.

The group still actively sells its literature, saying its main aim is to "bring people to the platform of understanding their original, constitutional position as an eternal servant of the Supreme Lord, Sir Krishna." The group estimates it has distributed approximately 400 million pieces of literature in the last thirty years, although the practice of mobbing people at airports and the like has now stopped. Prabhupada himself wrote 51 books, which have been translated into a wide variety of languages. Robert F. Corens, the director of the Washington Radha-Krishna Temple, feels the selling of literature is justified because: "many people are avoiding formalized religion, we distribute books in public, assuming that a beautiful, high-quality book will be taken home and eventually read. Sometimes the devotees are considered overly persistent in obtaining donations for the literature, although their tactics are no more aggressive than those of insurance salesmen."

Since reforming, making itself more open to public scrutiny and relaxing the rules for members who choose not to live in the temples, ISKCON has been attracting new followers again.

Chapter Three

UFO CULTS

SALVATION FROM THE STARS

I N 1947, KENNETH ARNOLD WITNESSED what came to be known as an "unidentified flying object," and the media frenzy about UFOs and extraterrestrial life began. While Hollywood poured out horror sci-fi movies, some people took the whole phenomenon more seriously and saw a link between what traditional religions always promised—the return of a messiah—and the visits of alien-driven flying saucers. If people have always looked to the skies for ultimate answers, perhaps they were justified in doing so.

Texts such as Ezekiel in the Bible refer to wondrous, fiery, sky-borne craft, as do ancient Indian sacred writings with their amazing, acrobatic sky-chariots, known as *vimanas*.

The advent of the millennium has led many people to look for answers to the eternal questions of who we are, where did we come from, and what is going to happen when we die? Traditional religions aren't seen to encompass modern attitudes, and while some people join established groups which attempt to impose solutions through anarchist activity, or others follow a self-proclaimed "messiah," some have found comfort and sense in groups which believe in—but do not necessarily worship—UFOs and aliens.

For members of these groups, life's answers are provided by extra-terrestrials. Although the majority of us would find this hard to swallow, it should be noted that followers of these types of groups tend to be well-educated and philosophical people who share a grave concern for the way that modern life is progressing. Whether they are striving for a positive future, as in the case of the Aetherius Society, or they feel isolated and ridiculed like the members of the tragic Heaven's Gate cult, they all feel the answer to their prayers lies somewhere beyond the earth's atmosphere.

The comet Hale-Bopp, which Heaven's Gate members believed was a "marker" or sign that the time had come to ascend aboard their exiting UFO.

THE AETHERIUS SOCIETY

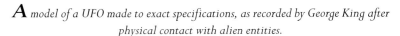

A model of a UFO made to exact specifications, as recorded by George King after physical contact with alien entities.

Billing itself as "a nonrecruiting organization," the Aetherius Society is one of the oldest and most respectable international UFO "sects." Formed in 1955 by Englishman George King, the society headquarters are still based in London. Dr King died in California on July 12, 1997, but the society continues his work, and membership is increasing with the renewed interest in the paranormal and new age concerns.

The society has a noble cause: it is "dedicated to the salvation and enlightenment of mankind." Members believe in a complex, spiritual system of interplanetary government overseen by the Great White Brotherhood and functioning on the continued production of spiritual energy. It is a belief system that has elements of Buddhism and new age thinking. Aetherians accept there are different astral levels, they actively practice spiritual healing techniques, and have a great affinity with ecological issues.

From 1954, King received hundreds of messages from what he quickly realized were beings from other planets, or what we would term "aliens." The first communication

he received was from a Master from Venus who called himself Aetherius—hence the Aetherius Society was formed. Over the years, King developed a close relationship with several entities who channeled information through him. He often went into trance-like states while the communications took place. The messages have been recorded for future generations.

Aetherius told King how the aliens—who are really just higher-level astral entities who take on a humanoid form when they visit earth—are part of a complex cosmic society which is run from the planet Saturn. The Cosmic Masters are extremely spiritual and in tune with what they call the Law of God, or the Law of Karma. They are thousands of years more spiritually advanced than humans on earth, and their understanding of karma has enabled them to leave their physical bodies behind. Whereas

KING DEVELOPED CLOSE CONTACT WITH SEVERAL ENTITIES

DR GEORGE KING

Born in Shropshire, England, in 1919, George King was brought up in an orthodox Christian atmosphere, but developed a deep interest in spiritual and psychic matters. Although not much is known about his early history, the Aetherius Society's biography of their "Cosmic Master" records how King became fascinated with yogic meditation, which he would practice for eight to twelve hours a day, despite holding down full-time jobs. King also developed his own psychic ability, which he felt was fine-tuned because of his deep understanding of meditation techniques. He channeled his psychic energy into spiritual healing, and believed he was "on the verge of discovering a new method of cancer treatment, which could cure certain forms of this malignant scourge," when he received a surprising message: "Prepare yourself! You are to become the voice of Interplanetary Parliament."

King established the Aetherius Society and its magazine, *Cosmic Voice*. He was and still is revered as a "true Yogic Master for the Aetherius Age"—after all, he was chosen by those we call "aliens" to pass on their message to us here on earth. King's dedication to the cause was unfaltering, even during his illness. Not long before his death, Dr Richard Lawrence told *Encounters* magazine how "he [King] is still on 24-hour standby, and has been since 1954. We don't think there is anyone else who for over 42 years has consistently been in contact on a weekly basis without a break." By "contact," Lawrence meant contact with aliens.

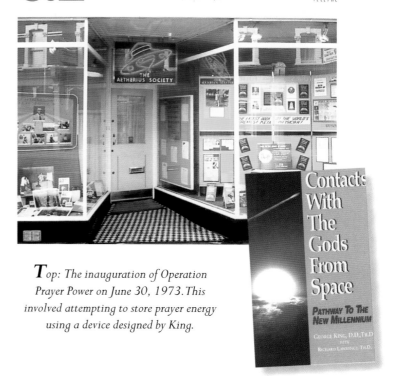

T*op: The inauguration of Operation Prayer Power on June 30, 1973. This involved attempting to store prayer energy using a device designed by King.*

THE SPIRITUAL PUSH

In July 1959, Sir George King channeled instructions from the Masters which were to send him on an incredible pilgrimage around the world. In what became known as Operation Starlight, King oversaw the charging of 18 mountains with intensive spiritual energy. He channeled the energy from the Masters until each mountain became, in effect, a giant storage jar of energy. The energy is to be used to help humanity through this difficult era in history. Members of the Aetherius Society still take pilgrimages to these centers of energy each year, despite the hardship of some of the climbs—one of the "centers" is at the top of Mount Kilimanjaro in Africa!

King invented various machines to collect, store, and release this cosmic energy to enable members to direct its healing properties into the most needy areas. Further missions followed, with names such as Operation Bluewater, which was directed at California, and Operation Prayer Power, which was a mass attempt to store prayer energy which could then be released later and directed at trouble spots. Aetherians still gather together and release this energy at times of crisis in the world.

At certain times of the year, since the Cosmic Masters contacted King, Aetherians have believed a giant spaceship comes into the earth's orbit. The dates are specific "windows" in their calendar, when this alien-crewed craft, called Satellite No. 3, transmits a giant energy beam, sending spiritual energy not only to key sites, but also to people who are already helping others. Much preparation takes place to receive this energy push, and Aetherian literature recommends that potential members experience prayer at these special times of the year, to be "amazed at the difference [it will] make."

humans only experience astral travel occasionally, either when they sleep or even more rarely when they have a near-death experience, the Cosmic Masters can lower their "vibrationary rate" so they can exist on other levels when they wish.

The Cosmic Masters are benevolent, and despite humanity's seeming determination to cause conflict and fight wars between the races, they want to guide us to a more peaceful and spiritual existence. King believed the Cosmic Masters had been helping humanity for years, sending prophets such as Buddha and Jesus to try to teach us the Law of God.

Our karmic history is such that we have now reached a crucial point in our evolution, and the Interplanetary Parliament has decided it is time for more direct action. This is why George King was contacted, and also why, since 1955, people have been reporting more UFO and alien sightings. The Cosmic Masters have been given permission to help avert the disaster they think we are heading for, and they channeled their plan for salvation to Dr King, who religiously recorded their wishes and advice, and now the members of the Aetherius Society are charged with carrying out the aliens' intentions.

Members are notably selfless, they tolerate other religions, and believe that by helping others they are spreading good karma and helping the planet's evolution. They believe all other worldly problems will be solved once mankind's karma is balanced, and treat the planet as if it is a living life force, even a goddess. The ultimate day of worship for Aetherians is July 8, when they spend the

KING LEFT
VARIOUS
PROPHECIES
BEHIND,
THE MOST
IMPORTANT
OF WHICH
PREDICTS A
"GREAT
COMING"

whole day in prayer, in deference to Mother Earth.

While they do not actively recruit new members, existing Aetherians do sometimes run lectures, such as the 1996 True UFO Contacts lecture tour in the UK, when they visited 18 towns and cities discussing the book Dr George King had written with European Secretary of the Society, Dr Richard Lawrence.

The publication, *Contacts with the Gods from Space: Pathway to the New Millennium*, is a thorough explanation of the Aetherius Society's principles and beliefs. New recruits don't have to give up any of their existing lives, or even change their religious beliefs, but they are expected to show an understanding of the Twelve Blessings and the Nine Freedoms—integral teachings channeled by the Masters. Master Jesus, who resided on Venus, according to King's writings, channeled the Twelve Blessings. The Blessings are an addition to Jesus's Sermon on the Mount, where He expands the original messages to include a more "otherworldly" slant.

Even though the aliens' main communication channel has now passed away, King left hundreds of instructions, prayers, messages, and prophecies which enable the society to continue functioning. There is no longer the "two-way link" that Richard Lawrence described when he was talking about their leader, but he made it clear that they have a well-established pattern of communication with the UFOs and Cosmic Masters. Prayer power is still collected and distributed, both on a one-to-one basis and in the case of more global problems.

King also left various prophecies behind, the most important of which is that there will be a "great coming," where the aliens will make their presence fully known. The date is undecided. Dr Richard Lawrence has alluded to Nostradamus's prediction of an "awesome lord" coming from the skies, but doesn't necessarily believe that 1999 will be when it happens. The Cosmic Masters won't visit until humanity is equipped to communicate spiritually on the same level, on a level that appreciates the interplanetary Law of God —that all our actions have far-reaching consequences and what comes around goes around—the Law of Karma.

ALIEN CONTACT

Because the Aetherians believe the earth is being looked after by Cosmic Masters, they also believe that the majority of UFO sightings are real. They are quite prepared for skeptics who ask why, if the aliens are so friendly, haven't they landed and introduced themselves already? The truth, according to King's channeled explanations, is that the cosmic entities must keep their distance because the majority of people are not ready to accept them yet, but this doesn't stop them watching over us.

They are allegedly not only protecting us from ourselves, by beaming positive energy at us, but also from other negative forces in the universe. While the Cosmic Masters are the true members of the Interplanetary Parliament, there are other entities inhabiting the astral realm who seem to act against us and promote feelings of fear. Aetherians don't believe they are the only people on the planet who have had contact with the aliens, but they do insist that Dr George King is the alien's true "voice." They are also skeptical about alien abduction claims, even though King himself claimed to have visited a spaceship. They don't believe that the aliens would harm us or allow other entities to hurt us in any way, so recently popularized accounts of forcible implantation and so on are fictional.

THE INTERNATIONAL RAELIAN MOVEMENT

Rael, formerly known as Claude Vorilhon, stands next to a model of a spaceship similar to one he has traveled on. The craft is one of the exhibits at the Raelian UFOland in Quebec, Canada.

In December 1973, Claude Vorilhon, a French sports journalist, was climbing in the mountains near Clermont-Ferrand in France when a spaceship appeared hovering above him. As he was the only witness, we only have his version of events—of how he met an alien being, and how he was consequently taken aboard a spacecraft and told he was to deliver the alien's important message to the rest of humanity.

Today, Vorilhon is known as Rael, and heads the International Raelian Movement from Toronto in Canada. The movement has approximately 40,000 members in 80 different countries world-wide. Full members voluntarily donate 10 percent of their salaries to the organization for the construction of an embassy where the "aliens" will one day convene with our heads of state. Rael makes it very clear that his followers do not support him financially. He still works as a writer, and is even an accomplished rally car driver.

In a series of books, such as *Let's Welcome Our Fathers from Space* and *The Message Given to Me by Extraterrestrials: They Took Me to Their Planet*, Rael recounts how the meetings with aliens took place, and outlines their plans for humanity.

It seems the aliens have decided we are at a stage in our evolution where we can finally handle the truth about our origins. Rael was told how the aliens, 25,000 years more advanced than ourselves, created humans in their own image by means of DNA modification. The aliens call themselves "Elohim," which Rael says is a word that has been misinterpreted over the centuries. In Genesis, the part of the Bible which explains humanity's creation,

FROM THE SPACESHIP A SMALL FIGURE WEARING A GREEN SUIT CLIMBED DOWN THE STEPS

"Elohim" has been translated to mean "God," but Rael says it is actually plural, and means "those who come from the sky."

Rael describes the first meeting with the Elohim in one of his books. A staircase was lowered from the spaceship, and a small, "childlike" figure wearing a green suit, with what has now become the Raelian symbol emblazoned on it, climbed down the steps. The alien told Rael he had been chosen as their contact because he was French, and therefore from a land where new ideas are readily accepted; he was a freethinker, he could communicate ideas simply to people, and finally, because he was born in 1946, after the bomb was dropped on Hiroshima, a major turning point in the world's evolution.

In a series of successive meetings with the little green man, Rael learnt that his mother, Marie Colette Vorilhon, was abducted and inseminated by the Elohim on December 25, 1945. Her memory of events was wiped clear by the aliens, and her son was born on September 30, 1946.

The alien told Rael that references to their work could

LIFE—BUT NOT AS WE KNOW IT

In a controversial move, Rael and a group of investors have set up a company called Valiant Venture Ltd which intends to offer human cloning to interested (and of course wealthy) parties. The company, which is already advertising its intentions on the Internet, will offer a service that it calls "Clonaid." Their advertising literature says: "This service offers a fantastic opportunity to parents with fertility problems or homosexual couples to have a child cloned from one of them."

The company, which is registered in the Bahamas, wants to set up a laboratory "in a country where human cloning is not illegal," but for the moment says it will subcontract the cloning to established scientific establishments. It has no ethical problems with the procedure because Rael teaches that life on earth was all cloned anyway by the Elohim. The cloning was possible because, according to Valiant Venture Ltd, the Elohim are 25,000 years more advanced than we are. The company even reassures prospective clients that Jesus's resurrection was actually "a cloning performed by the Elohim." Other services will also be offered, including Insuraclone, which means for a fee of approximately $50,000, Clonaid will safely store cells from individuals in case they die, and then create a clone of the person. This service is particularly recommended for parents anxious to safeguard their children. Even more bizarre is the "Clonapet" service, which although much less contentious since the cloning of Dolly the sheep in Scotland, is still causing apprehension among the scientific community.

How near Valiant Venture Ltd is to becoming the first human cloning company is open to speculation, but Rael's beliefs remove the major obstacle to the cloning debate—that of the moral issues involved. If the Elohim cloned us in their image, then the scientific knowledge needed to perform such experiments comes directly from them. Rael says: "Cloning will enable mankind to reach eternal life."

55

Dolly, the first animal clone, meets the press. Is the next step cloned humans?

OUT AND ABOUT

The International Raelian Movement still holds active recruiting sessions and arranges "Awakening Seminars," which are free to all members and are held in each continent once a year. Apart from these workshops led by Rael, the Raelian Movement is very active in individual countries. A Raelian news release is published for members, detailing what is happening in the movement world-wide, and it seems their most successful recruiting methods are through holding small seminars and selling Rael's books in the streets.

The International Raelian Movement hit the headlines in October 1997 when 150 of their European members joined a rally against intolerance of minority religious organizations by the German government. Moonies, Baptists, Scientologists, and other smaller groups demonstrated in Berlin. The Raelians were the only group who would march alongside the Scientologists, which ironically prompted some criticism of the movement, but Rael preaches religious tolerance and acceptance, although the Elohim believe religious doctrines can be repressive and encourage inhibitions.

be found in many ancient texts. Although they deliberately created us, the extraterrestrials left us alone to progress naturally. The only way the Elohim maintained contact with earth was through specially chosen prophets who were sent to guide humanity toward a more peaceful existence and toward the day when we would be advanced enough to accept our origins. Prophets such as Jesus, Moses, Buddha, and Mohammed were created to guide us in the ways of the Elohim. Rael believes he is the latest of these prophets, and he has been charged with a special mission. The Elohim have decided the time is right for us to face the truth about our past—the aliens want to come to earth and meet us all.

The aliens aside, Rael's message is not one of extremes. He teaches self-love, peace, and self-respect. Members continue living and working within the wider community, but are encouraged to get in touch with their more spiritual and sensual side through meditation. Eventually, money will be obsolete as machines and robots will "take over the menial chores such as food, clothes, consumer goods, and luxury production ... only then can creativity be really appreciated since people will not invent for commercial purposes, but for pleasure."

RAEL'S MESSAGE IS NOT ONE OF EXTREMES. HE TEACHES SELF-LOVE AND PEACE

Rael feels we have entered a crucial age where we have the scientific knowledge needed to destroy ourselves, but also, if we heed the Elohim's advice, we could use it wisely to become more like them. The Elohim have made it clear that the latter option is their hope for us. If the worst does happen, though, and there is a nuclear war, then according to Rael, the Elohim will intervene and save those humans who worked towards peace on the planet—whether they believed in the aliens or not. The Elohim are well aware of our many differences, and see individuality as a positive force, but they also teach that a universal understanding of their role in our future is necessary. To reach this end, the Elohim have instructed Rael to build an embassy where the aliens will meet world leaders and spread their message. The embassy will be a neutral meeting place to ensure no one particular earthly government looks as if it is being favored. Raelians will be at the embassy to welcome the Elohim and to ensure their visit is not a surprise (or shock).

SYMBOLS FROM THE STARS

*B*elow: A model of the proposed embassy
which will welcome the Elohim to earth so
they can meet world leaders and discuss the
future of the planet.

The Elohim's symbol is very important in the Raelian movement, for its design encompasses the whole theory behind the Elohim's message. All members wear the symbol, usually in the form of a pendant on a chain. It features a star formed from two triangles like the Star of David, with a "galaxy" in the center that represents "the cycle of infinity in time." The symbol of the Elohim is actually a Star of David with a swastika inside, but Rael changed the swastika for a less contentious sign.

The image of our galaxy as being infinite is all-important for Raelians, who believe everything within the universe is linked, from the smallest atoms to whole planets.

57

Plans for the embassy show it as a large, white building with a dome-shaped roof attached to another almost flying saucer-shaped section. It is not unlike a mosque in design. Raelians hope the embassy will be situated on land in Israel—holy land, which would be symbolic in welcoming our creators.

Although most of the money generated by the movement is to be plowed into the embassy scheme, the group has also funded another piece of architecture. UFOland in Quebec, Canada, opened to the public on August 31, 1997. It was built by Rael to the Elohim's specifications, and is billed as "the world's first interpretation center of UFO phenomenon." The building contains an exact copy of the spaceship that the Elohim took Rael aboard, as well as a 25-foot-high model of DNA. Other rooms have displays explaining how humans were created by cloning, the history of UFO sightings, and of course, a chance to experience Rael's teachings.

An area of Rael's teaching that has caused controversy is his belief in what he terms "sensual meditation." One of his books, which is subtitled *Awakening the Mind by Awakening the Body*, deals solely with this subject, which he says was a technique and series of ideas presented to him by the Elohim. Skeptics have described the "awakening" sessions as dubious, as they deal with sexuality in a group setting, but Rael sees "sensual" openness as an essential part of becoming more in tune with the universe. When the senses are heightened, then the mind is more willing to accept new experiences. It all sounds very new age and harmless, but there is, as one critic has pointed out, the "bathtub episode," which Rael recounts in *Beings From Outer Space Took Me to Their Planet*. In the encounter, a robot-making machine on the Elohim's planet "produces" six "perfect" girls for Rael, and they all share a very "sensuous" bath together.

HEAVEN'S GATE

Do and Ti, whose real names were Marshall Herff Applewhite and Bonnie Lu Trousdale Nettles, met in the early 1970s. According to *The Washington Post*, Applewhite admitted himself into a psychiatric hospital after becoming obsessed with his sexuality (some ex-cult members have suggested he was deeply troubled by a series of homosexual affairs). Although he told his sister he was recovering from a heart attack, he was in fact trying to "cure" what he felt was an illness.

Nettles was working as a nurse at the hospital, and had already developed an interest in "new age" teachings. She was in her early forties, like Applewhite, when they met and found that

A*bove: The Heaven's Gate website issues an ominous warning of the impending deaths.*

B*elow: Bodies are removed from Rancho Santa Fe, the group's San Diego villa.*

they both shared a similar brand of "theology." Applewhite always admitted that Nettles was the stronger of the pair, and it does seem that she convinced him they should form The Two and embark on a mission to "save" as many people as they could. They also convinced themselves that they were the two witnesses mentioned in the Book of Revelation in the Bible. True to the biblical account, they began predicting that they were prophets put on earth to save humanity, that they would be killed by their enemies, and that God would resurrect them after three-and-a-half days, taking them up to a higher level on a cloud. Apparently, the "cloud" was the biblical word for a UFO, according to The Two.

THE AWAY TEAM

When Deputy Sheriff Robert Brunk investigated the Rancho Santa Fe home of the Heaven's Gate cult on the afternoon of March 26, 1997, it was the smell that alerted him to the terrible tragedy. His back-up arrived shortly afterwards and helped uncover the 39 bodies that were found inside the San Diego villa.

At first the police assumed they were all male because their initial appearance was identical—all wore black shirts and sweat pants with new Nike sneakers, and they all had androgynous cropped hair. Further investigations revealed that 21 of the deceased were in fact women.

All but two of the bodies were covered in purple shrouds. Each had a carefully packed bag next to them, and a $5 bill and some change in their pockets. It was clear that the group thought they were going on some kind of journey. An arm badge had been sewn onto the sleeves of all their

shirts—it proclaimed its wearers as "Heaven's Gate Away Team."

Later, the police announced that a combination of Phenobarbital washed down with vodka and suffocation had caused the deaths. It seems the group died in "shifts," with the survivors cleaning up after their fellow team members had died and then placing the shrouds over the bodies. The last two to die, both of them women, committed suicide with no help and weren't wearing the purple shrouds.

Over a hundred videos were found at the ranch, most of which contained personal messages recorded in the garden by the cult members. On film, they spoke about feeling a sense of release and excitement about "exiting" their earthly vehicles and joining Ti on a higher level. They all made it clear that what they were about to do was of their own free will.

GOD WOULD RESURRECT THEM AFTER THREE-AND-A-HALF DAYS

The philosophy of the cult was a mixture of Applewhite's Presbyterian background and a fascination with UFOs, science fiction, astrology and astronomy. Although they developed their ideas over the years, The Two maintained their central belief that to be saved, individuals must forsake their human trappings, follow their strict teaching, and finally they would exit their earthly containers (bodies) and be taken to the higher level by a spaceship. The higher level was often equated with the Kingdom of God.

Applewhite and Nettles gained notoriety in September 1975 when a lecture tour led them to the tiny seaside town of Waldport, Oregon. For months before the meeting, posters had been appearing on telegraph poles stating: "If you have ever entertained the idea that there may be a real, physical level beyond the earth's confines you will want to attend this meeting."

Two hundred people attended the lecture that was held at the Bayshore Inn in Waldport. In the weeks that followed, 20 people tidied up the loose ends in their lives and joined the traveling cult that would become known as Heaven's Gate. Some disillusioned would-be members returned to Oregon after the UFO which The Two had promised, didn't arrive as planned. Most, however, left jobs, families, and homes to start a new life with the cult.

The Two had had limited success with their trans-American recruitment drive, mainly because would-be followers were told they must give up all their worldly possessions and cut all ties with their past. For most,

DO AND TI—OR WAS IT WINNIE AND POOH?

Do and Ti's reign as "Representatives from the Higher Level" took a variety of forms over the years. They initially called themselves The Two, then adopted the names Do and Ti after the musical notes. They variously called themselves other childish names such as Him and Her, Bo and Peep, Tiddly and Wink, and even more strangely, Winnie and Pooh.

Their cult acquired a series of different names before it became Heaven's Gate. In 1994, they called themselves Total Overcomers Anonymous, before that they had been HIM (Human Individual Metamorphosis), and various statements on the Internet referred to the group as the "Next Level Crew."

Members such as Chuck Humphrey, who made an unsuccessful suicide attempt in a hotel room in May 1997 when he was hoping to join his friends, are still spreading the Heaven's Gate philosophy. Small groups have been attending US college campuses and hosting meetings where they play the videos that Do made before he "left his container." Eerily, the members left behind almost all speak of regret at not joining the others, and they now call themselves "The Away Team."

although the idea of ultimate salvation by God's chosen Two and the promise of a ride on a spaceship was tempting, the demands of the cult were too severe.

The "disappearance" of the 20, together with the strange talk delivered by The Two, provoked a disproportionate amount of media interest. For the following sixteen years, the group maintained a low profile, moving their camps at least once a year.

At the same time as they hit the headlines for "alien abduction," both Applewhite and Nettles were linked to car theft and credit card fraud. Applewhite was charged, and served four to six months (accounts vary) in prison.

On his release, serious "training" began. The group was to be strictly celibate. If couples joined the group together, then they were separated. No physical attractions could take place, and each member had a "partner" who would watch out for "misdemeanors." Vanity was disallowed, and differences in gender were to be disguised. While it seems strange that the 39 bodies found at Rancho Santa Fe were so asexual, an even more

Do's Intro: Purpose - Belief

What Our Purpose Is - The Simple "Bottom Line"

Two thousand years ago, a crew of members of the Kingdom of Heaven who are responsible for nurturing "gardens," determined that a

*A*bove: *Publishing their beliefs on the Internet helped to recruit new members.*

*L*eft: *The group built an unfinished compound in Manzano, New Mexico, which they called "Earth Ship."*

SIX OF THE MEN, HERFF APPLEWHITE INCLUDED, HAD UNDERGONE SURGICAL CASTRATION

bizarre discovery was made during the autopsies which revealed that six of the men, Applewhite included, had undergone surgical castration. Unquestioning belief in the teachings of The Two was paramount—particularly that they all would die and then be ultimately resurrected.

A legacy of $300,000 bequeathed to The Two in the late 1970s enabled the group to establish itself in some comfort. They rented large properties in Denver and Texas, and began to prepare their souls for the arrival of the UFO.

In 1985, Bonnie Lu Trousdale Nettles died of cancer. The event didn't sit easily with the prophecies of The Two, especially when there was no miraculous resurrection. It seemed odd to cult members: if Ti and Do were aliens, as they had told their followers, and they had been sent on the same mission as Jesus Christ, then why had Ti died? Applewhite was distraught, but when some disillusioned followers left the commune, he once again redeveloped his philosophy. Beloved Ti had departed her "vehicle" because she had been called back to the Higher Level to prepare for the rest of the group's arrival. Do promised they would all join Ti very soon.

Coming out of virtual obscurity in 1994, Heaven's Gate paid a substantial sum for a large advert in *USA Today*. It warned that the time was drawing near, and urged people to get in touch with the group.

Although the 1994–1995 recruiting sessions were relatively successful, their public statements "outing" all Heaven's Gate members as aliens provoked a backlash of ridicule. Paranoia was rife. Members had cut themselves off from mainstream society as far as they could, only running their Internet design company, Higher Source, to pay the rent on the San Diego villa.

Applewhite began making references to Waco, and just in case the FBI raided them in a similar manner, a stockpile of guns was kept in the house. Statements about the cult, which they posted on the Internet, became more and more concerned with leaving earth, or "exiting." At about the same time, their UFO was spotted. Ti had telepathically informed Do that the UFO was following the comet known as Hale-Bopp. It was time to exit their earthly vehicles.

61

WHO JOINS A UFO CULT?

Of the 38 Heaven's Gate followers who committed suicide, most had cut off communication with their families almost totally. In the weeks after their deaths, relatives came forward with remarkably similar stories about how their sons, daughters and spouses had simply taken off and then only got in contact very rarely, usually via letters with no return address. David Cabot Van Sinderen was fairly typical of the group. He joined in 1976, when he was 27. His family saw him just four times during the following 21 years. They issued a statement after the suicides had been made public, saying: "while we did not completely understand or agree with David's beliefs, it was apparent to us that he was happy, healthy, and acting under his own violition."

While most families said their relatives seemed happy on the few times they had made contact, not all were convinced that they were making decisions of their own free will. Gail Renne Maeder, who was 28 years old when she died, joined after a series of personal problems in her life. According to her mother, when she joined the cult "her mind was controlled beyond her control." Edward Ernst, father of 40-year-old Erika Ernst, another Heaven's Gate victim, told the press how he had been trying to find his daughter for 21 years, and in that time they had only seen her once. He is convinced that the cult brainwashed Erika into committing suicide.

THE UNARIUS ACADEMY OF SCIENCE

Although groups with UFO-based philosophies have been growing since the 1950s, they also, with a few notable exceptions, tend to be relatively short-lived. Often, leaders who attempt to predict the date of a UFO landing or alien visitation will find that it is a risky business; this has led to the collapse of more than one sky-watching group when trusting followers find that these promises aren't fulfilled.

The Unarius Academy of Science was founded in 1954 by husband and wife team Dr Ernest L. and Ruth E. Norman, both of whom claimed to be Cosmic Visionaries. The group has developed a complex philosophy embracing a mixture of past-life therapy, extraterrestrials and UFOs, self-analysis, and new age thinking. At the very heart of its teachings are the beliefs that its leaders were and still are (Ernest died in 1971, but Ruth continues their work) in contact with higher spiritual beings who possess the answers to the earth's problems and who will stage "a 21st century cosmic event" when they land on our planet in 2001.

Unarius, which is an acronym for "universal articulate interdimensional understanding of science," is based in California where it has set up its headquarters and the Star Center, which helps members "tune into the subtle energies of a higher dimensional reality." It claims that members are helped on "the pathway of life to attain cosmic consciousness and to progress in their evolution to become way-showers and helpers to mankind still living in the darkness of the illusionary nature of materialism."

In simple terms, an interplanetary parliament of 32 planets believes earth is ready to become the 33rd

*T*he Normans claim to have lived together as husband and wife also in a previous life, as Jesus of Nazareth and Mary of Bethany.

member. One of the Space Brothers (entities very like ourselves but who have achieved a higher spirituality) told the Normans that "The spiritual leaders of the Interplanetary Confederation plan to land our craft upon your earth at a very auspicious cycle." Not everyone will be able to see the Space Brothers, only those humans who have opened their minds to a spiritual intelligence. The Unarius teachings help prepare their members by teaching them to accept the cosmos as a never-ending cycle which develops with time. Reincarnation, and the discovery of who individuals were in their past lives, is the key to attaining higher spirituality, and only then will the individual be ready to live on earth when it is accepted into the Confederation and begins to exist on a higher astral plane.

Ruth Norman's true spiritual identity, according to Unarius literature, is the Archangel Uriel. She is a representative of the spiritual hierarchy, and therefore technically a Space Brother. Her past lives include being Elizabeth I, Socrates, Peter the Great, and the last Inca of Peru, Atahualpa, and she has written a number of books explaining how, as an archangel, she has tried to influence mankind in the past.

Members are encouraged to "evolve positively" and by following Unarius teachings, attain "peace of mind and immortality of the soul." In this way they will become a full member of the Interplanetary Community, with the possibility that next time round they will be reincarnated onto a different planet. The group's literature suggests that the society has "reached" 500,000 people, although millions are following the same philosophy

GOD DOES DALLAS

The latest in a long line of apocalypse-prophecying UFO cults hit the headlines in March 1998, when Heng-ming Chen, the leader of God's Salvation Church and a respected professor, announced the end of the world was nigh. Printed on a sign outside a suburban ranch house in Dallas, Texas, were the words "God's Declaration," followed by the promise that God would appear at the house on March 31, 1998. Chen promised his 150 Taiwanese followers and the world's media that God would make a preliminary announcement on US TV's Channel 18 the week before his appearance, to prepare people for the incredible event.

The main purpose of his visit, Chen said, would be to reassure humanity that a fleet of spaceships would rescue everyone from the fast-approaching end of the world. Armageddon is due to begin, according to what God has told Chen, during February 1999, and will be triggered by a war in Asia. Like many doomsday prophets, Chen says the end of the world will occur because of nuclear explosions; he thinks everything will be over by 2043.

The UK newspaper *The Sunday Times* reported on March 15, 1998 that Chen guaranteed the appearance of God with his life. Under the headline "Flying saucer sect puts Texas on suicide watch," the article expressed fears that a no-show by God would result in a Heaven's Gate-style suicide, so determined were the God's Salvation Church followers. All professional people, the 150 had left important, well-paid jobs in Taiwan to join Chen, buying houses in the suburb of Garland, and donning the cult uniform of tracksuits and white cowboy hats.

When God didn't show up for the scheduled TV appearance, and then failed to visit 3513 Ridgedale Drive too, the cult quickly faded away. Chen wasn't quite so keen to court the interests of the media or journalists either, although he presumably still believes God is already amassing His squadron of flying saucers out there somewhere in preparation for the mass landing.

Surrounded by fellow cult members, Chi-Jen-Lo, aged ten, is described as "the reincarnation of Jesus."

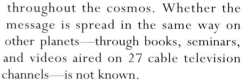

__A__bove: The Space Cadillac welcomes followers to the annual celebratory Interplanetary Conclave of Light.

__L__eft: The Star Center can help transport Unarius members to "visions of the future."

63

YALE COLLEGE
LEARNING RESOURCE CENTRE

throughout the cosmos. Whether the message is spread in the same way on other planets—through books, seminars, and videos aired on 27 cable television channels—is not known.

The Space Brother who refers to himself as "Your Brother in Light, Alta of Planet Vixall" warns that those of us who refuse to accept our higher spiritual destiny won't believe the mass landing in 2001, and therefore won't be equipped to live in our new interdimensional world. The arrival of "1,000 space scientists from the planet Myton" who will land on a raised portion of Atlantis in the Caribbean in 2001, will apparently vindicate all Unarius teachings.

ONE WORLD FAMILY

Noonan in the 1960s (below) and the 1990s (right) with his Family. Although the group has Utopian principles, they also have a precise political agenda.

64

NEW AGE AND PSYCHIC BELIEFS FIGURE STRONGLY

Allen-Michael Noonan founded the One World Family in 1966, in San Francisco. It followed a bizarre experience he allegedly had while at work. He was painting an advertising billboard when he was suddenly whisked away to another planet by aliens.

According to Noonan: "a shaft of ultraviolet light entwined with gold threads enveloped me, and I the entity in this body, was taken up into a great room inside a spaceship … as I transcended space and time into eternity, I saw the friends who are the guiding spirits of this earth humanity."

The organization has been variously known as the One World Family, the Messiah's World Crusade, or the less catchy Universal Industrial Church of the New World Comforter. Some skeptics have questioned Noonan's integrity, but the cult continues to exist in commune form, Noonan is still revered as its leader, and he is the only link that members have with the aliens.

In the familiar UFO cult scenario, Noonan preaches that he is the Messiah, and therefore the only person on earth who can truly receive messages from the extraterrestrials. In his case, the contact point is an alien called Ashtar, whom he met on his first visit to the spaceship when he was asked whether he would agree to be the savior of the world. How could he refuse? Ashtar communicates the extraterrestrials' philosophies, mainly adapting traditional Christian beliefs to incorporate an element of UFOs and a more advanced alien culture. Through Ashtar's teachings, Noonan has rewritten large portions of the Bible which he has gathered together in four volumes known as "The Everlasting Gospel."

The cult operates a series of health food and new age shops, despite their philosophy that "the big error is the

UFO ENCOUNTERS

Noonan says he had his first real contact with extraterrestrials in 1954. He has always believed he was different from other people, often seeing angels as a child and living in a bit of a dreamworld, but it wasn't until July 1954 that it all started to make sense for him. He had tried contacting aliens before, and says he was already aware that he came from the "Galactic Command Space Complex," which was trying to communicate with him.

A voice told him to follow "a great round cloud" to the desert, and constantly relayed directions until it told him to stop and set up a camp for the night. The next day, he was steered towards an isolated spot, because the extraterrestrials didn't want any witnesses, and then at about "10 a.m. the round

spaceship materialized about 6 feet off the ground, 75 feet away." Noonan describes the spaceship as being about 75 feet across with a large dome on top. At this point he wasn't allowed to get very close because his vibrations weren't in tune with the aliens. He conversed psychically with three entities, who told him they were called Favelron, Celeste, and Jameston, and he watched as they floated above the ground.

The purpose of this first encounter was to attune Noonan to the extraterrestrials' vibrational pattern so it would be easier and safer for his earthly body to meet with them again.

Right: The commune leader has appeared on TV and formed his own political party in order to promote Ashtar's teachings.

65

message of peaceful, more spiritual living to everyone, and the photographs of members all show large group shots of them looking healthy, hugging, and laughing. However, there are suggestions that the cult's peaceful proclamations have a more forceful hidden agenda.

Noonan, in some of his automatic writing that Ashtar channels, teaches that the One World Family will eventually take over the running of the US government and the United Nations. Far from being an empty promise, the cult's leader has tried to take his "Transcendental World Master Plan" to Congress. He heads a political party called the Utopian Synthesis Party, ran for governor of California in 1982, and even stood as a presidential candidate twice, in the 1980 and the 1984 elections—quite an ambitious resumé for a man who claims he was regularly visited by angels as a child, has been to Venus on several occasions, and teaches that he is "an extraterrestrial space being, incarnate in this body."

The Utopian Synthesis Party pledges to introduce a "real, autonomous, computerized, self-governing social system of free giving and receiving" where money will be phazed out and all debts and taxes will be abolished. A new social order based on a so-called 30/30 plan, where people work for 30 days then relax for 30 days, will make everyone into equal shareholders in the new society. All weapons will be abolished, criminals will be helped not punished, and government institutions will be disbanded. The new society will run, according to Ashtar, on a "one for all and all for one" basis.

backwards, ungodly usury money system," and they also publish books and videos, as well as appearing on US new age TV channels. Their communes are run on Utopian principles, where everyone is equal.

New age and psychic beliefs figure strongly within the commune, as members try to become more focussed on their "higher" purpose in the universe. It is only to be expected that followers of a man whose talents rely on channeling rather than tangible visitations would be keen to develop their own psychic abilities.

The aim of the One World Family is to spread this

Chapter Four

DOOMSDAY CULTS

PROPHETS OF ARMAGEDDON

THE APPROACH OF THE YEAR 2000 has raised a feeling of anticipation in the public consciousness. Prophets have been predicting the end of the world, or "Armageddon," for centuries, but for some reason, a new millennium seems to have created a growing tide of people proclaiming the end is nigh. This, coupled with the feelings of isolation, insignificance, and helplessness that the extremes of twentieth-century life place on us, has moved more and more people to find positive answers to their questions.

While it is easy to condemn the members as naive, it is more interesting to examine the motives and practices of their respective leaders. They formed what are termed by cultwatch groups "destructive cults," using techniques such as mind-control, physical abuse, fear, and enforced isolation to keep members loyal to them personally.

Although each of the five following doomsday cults followed a very different set of beliefs, each operated around the principle that the teachings of their own particular "guru" were not to be questioned. Often proclaiming a direct line to God, these leaders were then free to introduce whatever rules and practices they liked. David Berg, the controversial ex-leader of the Children of God, told his followers that sexual partners had to be shared with other members; David Koresh of the Branch Davidians went a step further and told his female followers that God had decreed they were to be impregnated with his own "seed." Money was central to Joseph Di Mambro and Luc Jouret's teachings, and the members of the Solar Temple allegedly funded a lavish lifestyle and an impressive network of property for their leaders. While some were content with controlling their own mini-empires, others, such as Shoko Asahara, guru of the Japanese Aum cult, strove for nothing less than world domination—what is most frightening, is that his plan could have worked.

*T*he appalling scene of almost a thousand dead bodies which greeted police officials at the supposedly "Utopian" Jonestown commune in 1978.

THE ORDER *of* THE SOLAR TEMPLE

Luc Jouret, a Belgian-born homeopathic doctor and registered obstetrician, headed the doomsday cult known as the Order of the Solar Temple. At the time of writing, 73 people linked to the cult have died, either through suicide or murder, but some experts believe the group lives on, and there is a chance more will give up their earthly existence to follow their guru.

The group was practically unknown until a series of events in October 1994 triggered a massive international police inquiry into the dealings of Luc Jouret and his partner in crime, Joseph Di Mambro. What followed has been a story full of intrigue, conspiracy, and unanswered questions. Various reports have linked the cult to the Mafia, to the death of Princess Grace of Monaco, to illegal gun smuggling, and to a complex money laundering operation. One of the biggest mysteries the police had to solve was how the deaths occurred, and why. Initial reports in the media spoke of mass suicides, but as autopsies were carried out, it became clear that not all the deaths were voluntary. It seemed that a substantial number of the bodies found were the victims of murder.

On October 4, 1994, five bodies were found in the peaceful town of Morin Heights in Quebec, Canada. They were all discovered in the same house, which had been set alight. Police soon realized that it wasn't accidental death when the bodies of ex-Solar Temple members Tony and Nicky Dutoit and their three-month-old baby son were found to have multiple stab wounds. They had been murdered. The two other bodies at the scene were also identified as Solar Temple members. Just as police linked the burning building to its owner Di Mambro, and investigations began into both the cult

*L*uc Jouret, whose obsession with the martyrdom of the Knights Templar led to his own followers suffering a similar death in flames.

leaders' whereabouts, reports came in from Switzerland of a mass suicide pact in the quiet resort of Cheiry.

The events surrounding the discovery of 47 bodies in two locations in Switzerland on October 5, 1994 are complex. Locals were amazed that something so dreadful could happen in their midst without them suspecting anything, but it soon became obvious that plans for the deaths had been taking shape for a while. Police were first called to deal with a fire at a farmhouse belonging to 73-year-old Albert Giacobino. It was around midnight when they arrived and found the body of the retired farmer. He had been shot in the head. An elaborately rigged firebomb device had only partially worked, and some rooms were left untouched. *Time* magazine reported how a firefighter came across "a chapel [inside the farmhouse] with mirrored walls and red satin draperies where 22 bodies lay, many cloaked in ceremonial white, gold, red, or black robes." The magazine reported that nearly all the dead had been shot, and most had been arranged in a circle among discarded champagne bottles. Ten had been suffocated.

Only a few hours later, a similar scenario was found in Granges-sur-Salvan, a small skiing village, also in Switzerland. This time the fires had been more successful and all 25 of the bodies would prove hard to identify. A group of three chalets had been rigged with gasoline bombs which were ignited by a ringing telephone. While the fires continued to burn, police realized that only two of the three bombs had detonated, leaving a potentially lethal situation for the emergency services. All 25 had to be identified by their dental records. Five of them were children. As more information came to light, it seemed that those involved in the deaths had all been members of

Right: Joseph Di Mambro, property dealer and cult leader, with his second wife Hélène.

Below: The bizarre farmhouse chapel where Templar-inspired rituals were performed.

IT'S ALL IN A NAME

Bizarre as it might sound, the whole series of suicides and murders could well have been triggered off simply because of a child's name. Tony and Nicky Dutoit had lived happily as members of the Solar Temple cult in one of the ill-fated Swiss chalets belonging to Di Mambro. Tony saw to the gardening and general repairs until he inexplicably fell out with the group. The husband and wife moved to Canada and had a son. It seems the couple's baby, who they called Emanuel, was the focus of Di Mambro's hatred. He dubbed the baby the "anti-Christ," and according to former cult members, he is likely to have ordered the killings. He believed the name was an insult to Emanuelle, his 12-year-old daughter, whom he considered to be a divine gift with great spiritual powers.

It is now thought that two of the dead who were found in Switzerland, Dominique Bellaton and Joel Egger, were responsible for the murders of the Dutoit family. Whether they knew they were flying back to Switzerland to their own deaths is unknown.

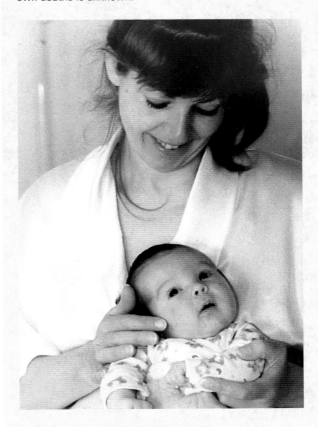

a cult called the Order of the Solar Temple.

Ex-members say it was Jouret's charisma that drew most of them to the group, although many now talk of the huge sums of money they parted with for the cause. Jouret taught that he was a reincarnated Templar Knight (some ex-members have said that Jouret believed, or at least told them, that he was the Son of God), that Di Mambro's daughter Emanuelle was a "cosmic child" conceived by immaculate conception, and that he could take them to a better place.

The "better place" that Jouret promised was actually in the Sirius star system, where he said a planet would be their new home. He predicted the end of the world would occur with a series of ecological disasters brought

The aftermath of the fires at the second cult death scene in the remote village of Granges-sur-Salvan, Switzerland.

PLAYING WITH FIRE

Luc Jouret's obsession with fire was ultimately realized with the skillfully rigged gasoline bombs that it is thought he helped construct. While the members were drugged, drunk, suffocating, or already dead, the simple ringing of the telephone would ignite the fuse and they would all descend to a new life in a ball of flames. He was obsessed with the martyrdom of the original Knights Templar who were burnt to death, and believed that the end of the world would be signaled by fire. He taught his followers that fire was magic and could perform transformations, incorporating alchemical philosophy with his strange predictions of apocalyptic doom.

about by corrupt governments, but that the Templar members would survive. Death was only "an illusion," according to Jouret—as long as they died in fire (an obsession of his), then they would survive to live in their new world.

Just over a year later, 16 more members of the cult died in south-east France. Three of the group were children, and police concluded that not all of the group had voluntarily committed suicide. Five more died in St Casmir, Canada, on March 20, 1997, although the number would have been eight had the three teenage children of one couple not persuaded their parents to let them live. It brought the total number of Solar Temple-related deaths to 73.

Little is known about what tied the group together. Members tended to be wealthy and highly educated. When the dead were finally identified, a former mayor, a journalist, and several well-respected businessmen were listed. At first, police thought Jouret and Di Mambro had escaped, but their bodies and those of their families were found to be among those at the Granges-sur-Salvan site.

Members maintained their jobs and lifestyles, only meeting up when they were summoned by their leader. Temple activities were kept secret, and the only active recruiting seems to have been carried out by Jouret and Di Mambro. Members were taught they were privileged, an elite in society who were privy to special knowledge. Total numbers of cult members are unknown, but it seems likely that there were no more than about 600, mainly in Canada, Switzerland, and France.

Jouret and Di Mambro met in 1978, when Jouret had already turned his back on conventional medicine and was practicing as an alternative healer. He also had a deep fascination with new age thinking. Di Mambro was 22 years his senior, and was already well established as a property dealer. He had dabbled in the occult, and was interested in secret societies, having formed a mystical group called the Golden Way, which Jouret joined. Together they founded the Order of the Solar Temple.

Little is known about their activities, but by the time of the first deaths, the cult was already under investigation. Jouret's message to his followers was becoming more and more obsessed with the end, being persecuted by the authorities, and the need to arm themselves. It had been this latter belief that had already got a few of the members into trouble. Three of them, including Jouret, had been charged with illegal arms possession, and various banks were becoming suspicious about the large amounts of money pouring in. It seems Di Mambro's business acumen had masterminded a complex money-laundering network, based around the ownership and sale of expensive properties. Journalist Michael S. Serrill, writing in *Time* magazine, suggested investigators thought the cult "may have amassed as much as $93 million."

SOME OF THE DEATHS WERE OBVIOUSLY NOT SUICIDE, SOME OF THE BODIES WERE BADLY BEATEN

While accounts differ as to exactly what the cult members believed and practiced, some surviving members allege Jouret was actually the third incarnation of Christ on earth. Rituals based on historical interpretations of Knights Templar practices were carried out in secret. The addition of robes, a strict hierarchy of office, and the promise that Jouret could lead them to be reborn was a potent mixture of doctrine that made the members of the Solar Temple cult feel somehow aloof from the rest of society. After all, they thought they knew that the world was about to end violently, and that they would be saved.

Although they were said to have had ultimate faith in both Jouret and Di Mambro, there remains the mystery of why some of the deaths were obviously not suicide. Not only were some of the bodies badly beaten, but investigators at the Cheiry site concluded that someone left the site after the massacre and took with him or her

PRINCESS GRACE AND THE SOLAR TEMPLE

On December 29, 1997, Britain's Channel 4 broadcast a TV documentary on Princess Grace as part of their *Secret Lives* series. The documentary suggested, citing evidence from a variety of sources, that the actress-turned-princess was involved with the Order of the Solar Temple. It was suggested that the Princess was initiated into the cult by none other than Luc Jouret and was then asked by Joseph Di Mambro to pay 20 million Swiss francs for the privilege. Interviewees, some remaining anonymous, tell of strange rituals involving sex and drugs where the Holy Grail would be "materialized" for members. The documentary also suggested that Princess Grace's death, in a car crash in 1982, wasn't an accident but was linked to her involvement with the Solar Temple cult.

the gun used to shoot some of the members. The weapon was later found after the fires had been put out at the scene of the second tragedy at Granges-sur-Salvan. It is also quite possible that at least some of those who died in 1994 didn't know they had traveled to Switzerland to die. Whether the deaths of the Dutoit family triggered the mass "exit" or whether Jouret and Di Mambro had been tipped off that various banks around the world had started investigations into their funds isn't known. Surviving members were as surprised as the rest of the world that their leaders had decided it was time to leave for a planet orbiting the Dog Star.

AUM SUPREME TRUTH

*J*apanese law enforcement officers use an electric saw to break into the main door of
Satian 6, one of the Aum's compounds near Tokyo, to arrest the cult leader Shoko Asahara.

On March 20, 1995, 11 or 12 commuters (sources vary) died horribly painful deaths when they were overcome by nerve gas on the Tokyo subway. Thousands more people had to be hospitalized. Suddenly, the cult known as Aum Supreme Truth had hit the world's headlines.

The cult's leader, 43-year-old Shoko Asahara, had ordered five of his trusted followers to approach the main business center from different directions on the subway. When the time was right, they were to release their special packages of deadly poison and cause one of the biggest panics Japan has known in modern times.

When the truth came out, that the Tokyo gas attack was only the beginning of Aum's sinister plans, it seemed hard to believe that such a dangerous group could exist without alerting suspicion, but Aum was under the control of some of Japan's brightest minds.

Asahara formed his cult in 1986, following what he said was a divine experience which showed him he must become a guru. He also had other, more earthly ambitions—mainly concerned with becoming rich. Toward the end, he alleged the cult had 40,000 members world-wide, but the number is probably nearer 10,000.

Asahara became obsessed with preparing for the end of the world, which he preached would come in 1997. His followers were warned that the USA would launch a nuclear attack on Japan, and the only people to be saved would be those who had prepared themselves fully—in other words, his disciples. Being "prepared" increasingly involved amassing weapons. Trips to Russia were frequent, and Aum found friends in high places by donating large sums of money to government-run organizations. The cult tried to buy automatic guns, ammunition, and tanks, and at one point tried to negotiate a deal for a MiG-29 fighter plane.

Even more sinister was the work going on within the secretive Aum compounds back in Japan. Local people in the area near Aum's biggest compound at the base of Mount Fuji were wary of the cult members. It was common for anguished parents to be seen pleading at the

SMALL ELECTRIC SHOCKS WERE DELIVERED TO CONNECT FOLLOWERS WITH THEIR LEADER

gates for news of their children, only to be sent away with nothing. Many members seemed thin and withdrawn, their meals were meager, in line with Asahara's wishes, and they were only allowed as little as three hours' sleep a day. Even more strange were the electronic "helmets" worn by most members. Their leader had decreed that members could only truly get close to his teachings when their brainwaves connected with his. By wearing tightly wrapped bandages with electrodes touching their scalps, small electric shocks were delivered every so often to connect the followers with their beloved leader. These helmets were essential for anyone considering salvation, and were available to rent if members couldn't afford the $70,000 required.

Money was central to the cult's thinking. All members donated their entire wealth to the cult, while books, initiation ceremonies, further rituals, and of course, the special helmets, all cost extra. Aum built up a massive business empire, most of which were companies used as fronts for the secretive scientific work going on behind the barbed wire of Asahara's compounds. Within his laboratories, bright young science graduates were trying to mix deadly biological weapons. It is hard to describe the horror that even one tiny drop of these gases can cause, but they are certainly effective killing machines. They attack the central nervous system of the body, causing major organs to shut off one by one until the heart gives up. Asahara is said to have had an obsession with Hitler's Nazi Party, and was keen to use their research into highly toxic gasses such as sarin.

When a ranchful of sheep were found gassed to death in the remote outback of Banjawarn in Australia and the strange Japanese men who had bought the farm disappeared, it didn't really warrant world headlines. Only later did locals realize that the sheep were the first victims of the cult's testing of nerve gas. The animals had taken only minutes to die. The ranch had been a perfect spot for uninterrupted trials.

Japan has the lowest crime rate of any democracy, so the subway attack on March 20 caused widespread panic. It wasn't long before police linked earlier reports of a sarin attack in the city of Matsumoto to the Tokyo one,

SHOKO ASAHARA

THE PROPHET IN PURPLE

Born in 1955 into a fairly poor Japanese family, Asahara became the only partially-sighted student at a school for the blind. It was there he developed his taste for leadership. When he left school, he tried various businesses selling herbal mixtures and acupuncture before he joined the "new religious" bandwagon.

The self-proclaimed Reverend Master of Aum Supreme Truth developed a fondness for wearing purple robes and sitting silently cross-legged while keeping a firm control over his growing empire. Reports from former Aum members would suggest that he is far from mentally stable. He would fly into uncontrollable rages if anyone looked like hindering his work, and then suggest incredible plots to seek revenge.

One of his most infamous suggestions was to launch lasers on the wedding of Japan's Prince Naruhito on June 9, 1993, which was to be attended by the most important world leaders. He was persuaded that the cult hadn't the capacity to produce lasers, but he insisted that the Japanese government must be taught a lesson. In the end, a car with a specially adapted tailpipe drove around Tokyo on the day of the wedding, releasing canisters of a home-made version of anthrax. It was sheer luck that the gas proved to be harmless.

73

Right: The Tokyo subway disaster.

Below: A cult member wearing the electronic headgear prescribed by Asahara.

and then from there to Aum. They quickly amassed enough evidence against the cult, which, knowing it would be implicated, issued a public statement to the press. Asahara said their cult was being set up by the government, which wanted to discredit it. Locals in the region of the Kamikuishiki retreat near Mount Fuji reported a mass of comings and goings at the cult compound, presumably as members tried to dispose of the evidence.

Despite their efforts, police were amazed at what they found when they raided the headquarters on March 22. There was no big showdown, despite fears of a Waco-style clash with police. Cult members shouted at the officers, but let them get on with the task of cutting through the doors and breaking open padlocks. The first in wore protective suits, in case fatal chemical gases were released.

About fifty members of the cult were found suffering from malnutrition, some being so heavily drugged they had no idea where they were. Other members were

ABOUT 150 AUM MEMBERS WERE ARRESTED ON MINOR CHARGES

found in the punishment blocks, weak from beatings and experiments carried out by the cruel Dr Hayashi's medical team. One man was found to have had part of his brain removed in a botched experiment. Officers also came across the chemical manufacturing equipment, stock-piles of weapons, and the infamous "incinerators" which were used to destroy the evidence of a still unknown number of murders.

About 150 Aum members were arrested on fairly minor charges, while investigations continued into the leaders of the cult. In Japan, people are very rarely arrested unless their guilt is almost certain. It took until May 16, when police raided 130 Aum-linked properties, for the guru himself to be arrested. As more and more members came forward, filling in the gaps of Aum's

*P*olice raid the Aum chemical plant, its network of pipes clearly visible.

history, became clear the cult was linked with other atrocities. The cult was responsible for the murder of an anticult lawyer, Tsutsumi Sakamoto, and his wife and child. They had also carried out other sarin gas attacks, and were responsible for numerous assaults, intimidation, and even further murders.

Asahara is currently serving life imprisonment, as are a number of high-ranking Aum members. The cult's funds ($10 million were found in Asahara's personal safe, along with a substantial amount of gold) were confiscated, although the cult wasn't officially declared illegal, as it was considered harmless now its leaders were all locked up. However, Asahara has apparently revised the date of Armageddon to 2001, and there are recent reports that the cult is growing in numbers again. Members are operating a chain of computer stores, and have allegedly opened a training hall in Tokyo. Local branches of the cult

are also said to be reforming, and Asahara is still held to be the cult's savior, his erratic teachings being passed on to a group who still believe his apocalyptic predictions.

Japanese officials still keep the group under very tight surveillance, which is probably highly advisable, considering in 1995 they had manufactured enough lethal gas to kill potentially millions of innocent people.

ASAHARA'S MOST WANTED

Dr Ikuo Hayashi

Dr Hayashi (below), a registered heart surgeon, received a life sentence on May 26, 1998 for his part in the Tokyo subway attack. David Kaplan and Andrew Marshall describe Hayashi as "the cult's own Joseph Mengele" in their book *The Cult at the End of the World*. Hayashi was in charge of Aum medical services, and was responsible for using an unknown number of humans in experiments. His "failures" were simply burnt in the compound's huge incinerator. He told the court he hadn't thought the sarin gas was that dangerous, and only escaped the death penalty because he showed some remorse for his actions.

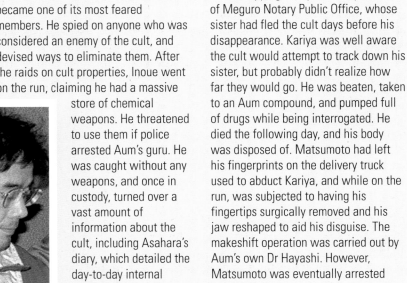

Yoshihiro Inoue

Inoue made it to the rank of Minister of Intelligence inside Aum's hierarchy. He joined the cult when he was 18, and became one of its most feared members. He spied on anyone who was considered an enemy of the cult, and devised ways to eliminate them. After the raids on cult properties, Inoue went on the run, claiming he had a massive store of chemical weapons. He threatened to use them if police arrested Aum's guru. He was caught without any weapons, and once in custody, turned over a vast amount of information about the cult, including Asahara's diary, which detailed the day-to-day internal running of the cult.

Takeshi Matsumoto

Matsumoto was one of Japan's most wanted in March 1995. He was linked to the kidnapping of Kiyoshi Kariya, head of Meguro Notary Public Office, whose sister had fled the cult days before his disappearance. Kariya was well aware the cult would attempt to track down his sister, but probably didn't realize how far they would go. He was beaten, taken to an Aum compound, and pumped full of drugs while being interrogated. He died the following day, and his body was disposed of. Matsumoto had left his fingerprints on the delivery truck used to abduct Kariya, and while on the run, was subjected to having his fingertips surgically removed and his jaw reshaped to aid his disguise. The makeshift operation was carried out by Aum's own Dr Hayashi. However, Matsumoto was eventually arrested on May 18.

Millions of people world-wide watched their TV screens as the Waco compound exploded into flames.

THE BRANCH DAVIDIANS

One of the most alarming moments in modern history took place in the otherwise nondescript town of Waco, Texas. On February 28, 1993, the US government gave the Alcohol, Tobacco and Firearms Department permission for over a hundred of their officers to raid the headquarters of a little-known religious community in Waco. Now the name of the place will be forever linked to David Koresh and the massacre that followed a 51-day siege at his compound. Even today, the event retains an air of mystery. Conspiracy theories abound, and rightwing organizations accuse the US government of incompetence—and even worse, perhaps orchestrating the showdown to warn the growing number of Militia groups that the FBI is prepared to act.

The truth is probably a little less sinister, although most impartial commentators have now admitted that the FBI's handling of the siege could have been better organized. In the end, Waco was a tragedy from which only 9 out of 96 members managed to walk out alive. Not one of the highly trained negotiators, let alone the fear of force, was enough to convince Koresh to surrender and let the ATF raid his ranch in search of illegal weapons.

Tragically, it was only after the event that the world became aware of just what sort of man David Koresh was—a man obsessed with his own sexuality, who not only practiced polygamy, but had sex with underage girls, and taught that women who snubbed his teachings were to be raped. Koresh was also a cruel man, clever and manipulative, but ultimately selfish and paranoid. He was greedy for power and soon became a dictatorial prophet.

Koresh, known as Vernon Howell before he changed his name, didn't found the Branch Davidian group. It has a long history, dating back to 1935, when Victor Houteff,

HOWELL BECAME LOIS RODEN'S LOVER. SHE WAS 68 YEARS OLD

a Bulgarian immigrant, broke away from the Seventh Day Adventist Church and formed the more fundamentalist Shepherd's Rod. The group moved to Waco and formed a tight-knit community until several years after Houteff's death, when his wife, the then leader of the group, predicted the second coming of Christ in 1959. When the year passed by uneventfully, the Shepherd's Rod followers quickly doubted their leader's authority, and many left to form splinter groups. The charismatic Benjamin Roden founded one of these groups. He called his group the Branch Davidians, after the biblical King David.

When he died in 1978, Roden's wife Lois succeeded him. Both ran the group as if they were prophets, reinterpreting the Bible after having visions and dreams. The emphasis on being saved from Armageddon appealed to the 24-year-old Vernon Howell, who joined in 1983 after falling out with the mainstream Seventh Day Adventist Church.

Reports differ as to how it happened, but Howell became Lois Roden's lover. She was 68 years old and the controller of an influential Christian group. Martin King and ex-Branch Davidian member Marc Breault wrote a fascinating account of Howell's takeover in *Preacher of Death*. In the book, they claim Howell became besotted with Lois because of her influence and contacts, and seduced her by telling her it was God's will they had a child together.

The sexual relationship between the two caused yet another rift in the group. Lois's son, George, fearing that Howell would inherit the group (and their finances), launched a hate campaign and tried to drive the younger man away. Over the next few years, open hostilities broke out while members had to choose which prophet they believed. In the end, Howell won when George was commited to a mental institution

THE HOUSE OF DAVID AND THE BRIDES OF CHRIST

David Koresh wasn't the first cult leader to use his hold over members to satisfy his own sexual needs, but unfortunately, he didn't just prey on vulnerable adults. Rachel Jones became Koresh's "legal" wife aged 14, after he had had a sexual relationship with Lois Roden. Although it seems Rachel was devoted to the tall, powerful leader, Koresh wasn't satisfied, and surrounded himself with a group of women who became known as the "House of David" or the "Brides of Christ."

Koresh justified his affairs by preaching to the group that as the Son of God, he must spread his seed—and he did. He not only took the younger women of the group as his lovers, and instructed male members to give him their wives, but had ongoing sexual relationships with girls as young as 12.

In fact, Rachel's own sister became Koresh's third "wife" when she was just 12, and bore him a daughter. Marc Breault, an ex-member of the cult, talks of Koresh's relations with the younger girls with disgust. They believed it was their duty, and probably an honor, to sleep with their prophet, but Breault says Koresh was well aware of the risks. In *Preacher of Death*, Breault says Koresh confided, "I'll be put in jail for this one day," when he was talking about his underage nocturnal activities. He never was, and most of the "wives" perished with him in the flames of Mount Carmel.

THE TANKS GO IN

On April 19, 1993, after many hours of failed negotiations and broken promises by the cult, the FBI decided to storm the Mount Carmel compound. Just after dawn, the chief negotiator called the cult and told a leading member that the FBI planned to end the siege. They also told the cult what they intended to do. The FBI later said that they didn't believe Koresh would sacrifice himself or his followers, but there was great criticism of their heavy-handed tactics.

As the tanks rolled in, knocking holes in the compound walls through which tear gas was thrown, it wasn't just the FBI who watched. TV pictures were being beamed live all over the world. No one expected what happened next. As negotiators pleaded with the cult members to come out, hoping maternal instinct would lead to at least the mothers and children fleeing the gas, fires broke out in various sections of the compound.

It was a windy day, and the fires spread quickly. Reports say there was a series of massive explosions as the flames met the stockpiles of ammunition and fuel stored inside the buildings. The world watched, hoping people would come running out, but only nine escaped. The rest of the bodies were recovered by a shell-shocked group of officers and paramedics when the explosions had finally stopped.

IT WAS GOD'S WILL THAT HE SPREAD HIS "SEED" WITH AS MANY WOMEN AS POSSIBLE

after a bizarre fiasco where he tried to prove his religious devotion by attempting to restore life to a member who had been dead and buried 20 years.

Not long after he began his affair with Lois, Howell announced that God came to him in a dream and told him to "marry" the 14-year-old daughter of members Perry and Mary Bell Jones. The parents gave their consent, and their daughter Rachel was given to Howell. She quickly became pregnant and bore him a son. Rachel was the first of many of Howell's "wives," although at this point in his career he was putting most of his energies into becoming the leader at Waco.

It seems that with the absence of George Roden from the scene, and the death of Lois, Howell took control of the group. It was under his fanatical and warped teachings that the group evolved from a reclusive Christian organization into a world-famous cult. Life was harsh for group members, and became increasingly so as Howell's need for power took over. He renamed himself David Koresh—David because of King David, and Koresh because he said it meant "death." Food was rationed, and Koresh developed obsessions with various types which were or weren't to be eaten. The children were treated especially harshly, being beaten for the slightest misdemeanor. One of the main reasons the FBI wanted to storm the compound was the reports from ex-members of both physical and mental abuse against minors.

As well as stockpiling weapons—which, bizarrely, Koresh obtained legally because he had a gun-trading license—all members of the cult were expected to train physically for the day when they would face their final challenge. Long hours of physical exercise were followed by even longer hours of Koresh's heady preaching. Men and women were segregated, and even married couples were often forbidden to even talk to each other. Their loyalty must be to Koresh alone. He justified his extraordinary behavior by telling his followers that he was God's seventh messenger—the prophet who had been told the final outcome for humanity—so when he said it was God's will that he spread his "seed" with as many women as possible, most complied. Those who didn't were brutally punished or hounded from the cult. By

Only a handful of cult members survived unscathed from the Mount Carmel compound, to be arrested later by police officials.

1994, what had started as a peaceful religious organization had turned into a paranoid cult with a leader who couldn't control his own sexuality and had developed an obsession with becoming a rock star. Surviving members have told how Koresh would play endless concerts of his music to them, how he went through a phase of worshiping Madonna as the most perfect woman alive and tried desperately to be accepted by the music industry. Members of his band also tended to hold the most respected positions within the cult.

Armageddon came sooner for the cult members than most had thought. Koresh had always preached that Judgment Day would happen after they had all moved to Israel. He would then be called upon to instruct who should be saved. But when the ATF arrived with search warrants, they were also armed with allegations of child abuse and details of Koresh's harem of underage girls. Koresh wasn't going to let go of his power that easily. The search warrants were refused with a barrage of bullets that left four ATF agents and six cult members dead. Sixteen other agents were wounded.

In the following stand-off, the ATF and FBI cleared the area surrounding the compound and circled the buildings. Officials were joined by the media; enterprising locals selling food, drink, and even T-shirts; tourists; religious sympathizers; and paramilitary groups who harangued the government forces. Loud music was blared out of high-powered speakers, and the cult's electricity and phones were cut off, in efforts to make things so uncomfortable that they had no choice but to surrender.

Twenty-one children and a few adults were released over the 51 days, but the ATF were well aware there were still children in the compound, and that some cult members were suffering from gunshot wounds. An intolerable waiting game was played out, during which Koresh made TV broadcasts, consulted a lawyer, and told negotiators that he wouldn't come out until he had finished writing a religious text.

In the end, according to the US government, worries for the safety of the children decided the issue, and the order to move in was given. When the bodies, most of which took weeks to identify, were formally listed, Koresh's and those of 13 of his children were among the remains. Koresh had shot himself in the head. Other cult members bore gunshot wounds, but it still isn't clear whether they committed suicide or were shot trying to escape from Mount Carmel.

THE PEOPLE'S TEMPLE

Over 900 members of the People's Temple cult are thought to have died in what was initially called a "mass suicide pact," at a jungle retreat in Guyana in November 1978. The carnage was recorded for posterity on a voice-activated tape recorder placed under the chair of the cult's leader, the Reverend Jim Jones. When investigators played the tape back, apart from the general sound of mayhem, gunshots, and screams, Jones's voice could be clearly heard as he yelled into a loudspeaker, telling his congregation that it was time for "White Night."

Jim Jones, a self-proclaimed messiah, led a 1,200-strong congregation to the remote region in Marxist Guyana in 1977. His idea was to set up a communist-based Utopian society that promoted racial tolerance and rejected the excesses of capitalism. The reality of what went on at the commune is still shrouded in mystery, and conspiracy theories abound, but at least one modern commentator has compared it with a concentration camp. Whether it was quite that horrific remains open to interpretation, but Jonestown, as it came to be known, was no Utopia. For the almost one thousand people who perished there, it proved to be their downfall.

Jones started his career in religion when he was just 12. He enjoyed preaching to his friends at school, but at this stage it was mostly evangelical Christian theology. It was only later that he enmeshed his religious beliefs with an avid passion for Marxist principles.

Jones set up his first Church in Indianapolis when he was 18, with his new wife, Marceline, and began studying other religious leaders, to adapt their style. He famously had a door-to-door salesman job selling, of all things, monkeys, to raise the funds he needed to maintain his Church. In 1955, he founded the People's Temple, which quickly gained notoriety—and consequently new members—because of Jones's "hands-on" healing

sessions, where he would extract cancerous growths and other visible ailments from members who came for help.

Despite these rather distasteful hoax healings, Jones became quite an influential figure in the community. He and his wife had adopted children from different racial backgrounds, which he called his "rainbow family." In 1959, he set up a fund for orphanages under the same name. He also became linked with projects fighting poverty and racism in the area, working with soup kitchens, restaurants, and clothing stores for the poor, and also more militant groups fighting for access to proper educational and medical facilities for people living in ghettos.

Jones reached the status of becoming chairman of the San Francisco Housing Authority in 1976, was appointed director of an Indianapolis human rights commission, and is even alleged to have had lunch with President Carter's wife, Mrs Rosalyn Carter.

Jones's critics were beginning to catch up with him, however, and despite the public face of a humanitarian evangelical preacher, allegations of fraud, both monetary and as a healer, were circulating. His free drug-rehabilitation center was being accused of handing out phoney cures for illnesses as serious as cancer. Jones became increasingly paranoid about the US authorities, probably because of his long-standing affiliation with the US Communist Party, and after a series of attacks on one of his buildings, decided to look elsewhere for a base.

The 300-acre commune was set up in the middle of inhospitable rainforest, 140 miles from the capital of Guyana, Georgetown. It seems that initially Utopia was almost achieved. The forest was cleared, in harmony with the local inhabitants, and the whole population worked to build the neat rows of brightly painted cottages, workshops, and farming buildings. There was a hospital, a main square near Jones's quarters, and even an open-air

The bodies of parents and children were found huddled together after the mass suicide at the Jonestown commune in Guyana.

Right: When police were alerted to what had happened at the jungle hideaway, they found evidence of mass poisoning, strewn among the bodies.

JIM JONES

Jones was born in Lynn, Indiana, on May 13, 1931. He was of mixed race, a blend of Native American and white cultures, and throughout his life he maintained a strong, almost obsessional preoccupation with racial issues. He married a nurse, Marceline Baldwin, on June 12, 1949, when he was only 18 years old. The two adopted seven children into their "rainbow family," and Marceline remained faithful to her husband's teachings. Her body was found next to his at Jonestown.

Many ex-members have attested that the leader started out with good intentions, and that he was an inspiration, but somewhere along the line his philosophy on life got twisted and out of control. It is thought that by the time things started to go wrong at Jonestown, Jones was addicted to an alarmingly high daily dose of drugs, mainly stimulants and sleeping pills. This would certainly explain his paranoia that the commune was under threat from capitalist enemies.

pavilion where members would sit for hours listening to the ideology of their leader.

One of the few surviving Jonestown members, Tom Bogue, who was 17 at the time of the massacre, told reporters from *The Washington Post* that he had been at the commune for about two-and-a-half years. Up until a year before the tragedy, life had been pleasant, "where everyone had lots of freedom," but about twelve months before, Jones had started "acting crazy."

JONESTOWN, AS IT CAME TO BE KNOWN, WAS CERTAINLY NO UTOPIA

Jones developed a theory of "Translation," in which he predicted the end of the world via nuclear war, and that he and his followers would all die, but would be taken to another planet for a better life. About the same time, he made all the members prepare for this ultimate end by taking part in what amounted to rehearsals for a mass suicide. Every couple of weeks or so, members would be subjected to long, frantic rants about persecution and their enemies, then they would be expected to drink from cups handed out by Jones's ever-present security guards. They were told the cups contained poison. Parents were instructed to inject the liquid into their infants' mouths.

In a horribly predictable manner, what was once a respectable evangelical Church had turned into a confused cult led by a fanatical leader. Anxious family members were already contacting the authorities back in the US, full of stories of kidnapping, financial fraud, and worse. Although not much is known about Jones's sexuality, some ex-members have alleged he demanded that all followers be receptive to his advances, whether they were male or female. They were certainly asked to cut ties with their spouses.

Punishments were severe, as were stories of what would happen to deserters. As members had handed over all their belongings to Jones, there was no way to escape the compound except to chance it in the hostile jungle, and not many were that brave. The few survivors who spoke of that last terrible year described an "extra care unit" which administered all manner of drugs to members to keep them under control, and a disciplinary method known as the "punishment box," where so-called offenders were kept locked up in a tiny box until Jones believed they were sorry. It was common for escapees to be put in chains and made to work incredibly long hours in the sweltering heat, and Jones's team of armed security guards always patroled the whole community.

82

After Congressman Ryan's visit and eventual murder on November 18, 1978, Jones went berserk. He called all his followers together, and told them it was time for "White Night." The medical team mixed a cocktail of a soft drink laced with tranquilizers and cyanide, and placed the vat on a table in front of an altar that Jones had constructed. What happened next is legendary.

According to one member who managed to survive the experience, Jones ordered parents to kill their children first by making them ingest the mixture, then lie down and drink the cocktail themselves. Undoubtedly, some members obeyed their leader until the last, believing the end of their Utopian world was nigh, but it seems that others who objected to the plan were forced to drink, or were injected with poison. Others who tried to flee were shot or forced back at

THE CONGRESSMAN'S VISIT

The catalyst for the November 1978 massacre that shocked the world was a visit to the remote site by a concerned US Congressman. Leo Ryan was disturbed about the human rights abuses that he had heard might be taking place at Jonestown, and decided to visit the place himself. Ryan took along a team of journalists, lawyers, and a few concerned relatives, in two light planes that landed at the small airport of Port Kaituma. They were met by angry cult members who were annoyed by the interference of outsiders.

Despite Jones's open hostility toward the Congressman, it seems that the visitors were impressed with the self-sufficiency of the cult. They left after spending the day in the jungle society, telling the cult that their reports would be by and large positive. It was only when a few members expressed a wish to join the visitors and leave the cult that things turned nasty. One of Jones's henchmen tried to stab the Congressman as he left, but was pulled off. Jones's paranoia grew unbearable. He ordered a team of devoted followers to trail the group back to the planes and make sure they didn't leave. Seven of the group were shot dead: Ryan, three journalists and three people who were trying to flee the cult. Others were wounded or escaped into the jungle. It was now only a matter of time before Jonestown was investigated. "White Night" was nigh.

gunpoint by the guards, who later killed themselves. The cyanide only took about five minutes to work, so in a short time the jungle was silent.

Bodies lay haphazardly all over the compound. Families lay together with their arms around their children, and Jones himself lay on his altar, killed by a single shot to his head.

As the few escapees, including two US lawyers who had not tried to leave with Congressman Ryan, managed to make it through the jungle, shots and screams rang out around them. They desperately tried to reach a town to get help, but by the time any authorities made it back to the commune, the place was silent and its floor was a carpet of limp bodies.

Initial reports estimated the number of deaths at 408, but this was later revised to 913. The whole event caused such a shockwave through the small country of Guyana that initially procedures weren't carried out properly, and the bodies were left for two days in the sweltering heat. By that time, they were so badly swollen with gasses that it was difficult to try to identify them, let alone work out who had died voluntarily and who had been murdered.

Over half a million dollars were later uncovered at the Jonestown commune, along with a treasure chest of gold and bankers' checks. Further investigations revealed that Jones had a number of foreign bank accounts, and was effectively a multimillionaire.

The heat and humidity of the jungle made it impossible for the authorities to identify all the bodies of the victims.

CHILDREN OF GOD

Although in recent years the Children of God organization, which now calls itself The Family, has radically restructured its organization, the original cult is still remembered as one of the most controversial and destructive of all.

David Berg founded the Children of God in 1968, when he went with his wife and two eldest children to help his evangelist mother run a coffee-house for dropouts in California. The crowd who frequented the beach-side center were mostly young people caught up in the rebellion of the 1960s hippie movement. They were disillusioned with mainstream politics and society, felt their parents didn't understand them, and were looking for a new direction in life. Berg appealed to their way of thinking. He played the guitar and preached on the beach his own special brand of Christian evangelism which rejected the establishment of education, the Church and parental control, but embraced the free-love philosophy that the young people wanted to hear.

In 1969, a group of fifty or so followed Berg to Arizona, and then on to Texas, where they set up a commune on radio evangelist Fred Jordan's ranch. Berg renamed himself Moses Berg, and the now 2,000 members referred to him as "Mo." His fundamentalist Bible interpretations began to take on a more unusual slant as his self-importance grew. He saw himself as a "prophet of the endtime," at various times predicting that California would slide into the sea, Jesus would return in 1993, and that there would be a massive communist takeover of the United States which would lead to all Christians being persecuted. His prophecies were channeled through him from a variety of sources, mainly a thousand-year-old Gypsy king

called Abrahim, but Berg also claimed to be in contact with Joan of Arc, Rasputin, and Merlin the magician.

Members signed a Revolutionary Contract, handing over all possessions to the movement and promising to cease contact with friends and family. The only time parents were generally approached was when the group needed money. For this purpose, files were allegedly kept on all the parents' financial situations. Once they joined the communes, most lived in poverty, sometimes resorting to stealing food from local supermarkets. Money was raised by selling group literature on street corners. Berg lived apart from his communes, maintaining a form of mystique, and communicating by sending an increasingly bizarre series of sermons which members called the "Mo Letters."

The first Mo Letter explained why the "prophet" had moved another woman, "Maria," into the family home—because Jane, his wife, represented the old Church, and Maria was the new. Berg's personal obsession with sex soon permeated the ranks of the whole group. By 1978, it wasn't just Berg who got to share the wives of other members, it was the "Law of Love" that the women should be shared among all members. The Mo Letters became increasingly frank, were often illustrated with sexual images (sometimes with pictures of Berg himself and various women), and began advocating lesbianism, homosexuality, and group sex, allegedly even legitimizing incest. One of Berg's own

HOOKERS FOR JESUS

"Flirty fishing" (or "FFing" as it was known in the group) is probably what most people remember about the Children of God cult. Both female and male members were instructed to entice new members to join by going to bars, clubs, and even joining dating agencies, and carrying out "Sex for Jesus." Berg issued a "Flirty Fishing Handbook," in which he called his women "God's Whores," or "God's Witches." The press dubbed them "Hookers for Jesus." According to the guide, women should dress in low-cut tops, go bra-less, wear makeup, and comply with any of the "fish's" desires. They were also to make it clear that their attention didn't come free. In effect, they prostituted themselves because Berg told them it was God's will.

Quite apart from the spread of sexually transmitted diseases, there was the problem of illegitimate children. Contraception was banned by the cult, so it was inevitable that with so much "sharing" going on, pregnancies would be commonplace. It was not unusual for women to have five or more children, all of whom had to be brought up on the meager rations of the communes.

Below, center: David Berg, who has inspired young followers in the 1960s (left) and the 1990s (below) to preach his evangelical message.

BY TAKING PART IN THESE ACTS THEY WERE PASSING ON GOD'S LOVE

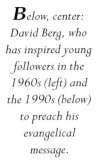

daughters, Linda, left the cult and wrote a damning book about her father, alleging he had abused one of her sisters and encouraged sex with underage children. The Mo Letters themselves were rarely specific, most just made suggestions, but the language was generally highly sexually charged, and Berg justified his desires by assuring his followers that by taking part in these acts they were expressing and passing on God's love.

When a group of concerned parents got together and formed FREECOG to try to publicize the damage they thought the cult was doing, the authorities in the USA and UK also became interested. Berg instructed members to withdraw to less oppressive nations, warning that the two countries would be wiped out by nuclear war. The advent of Aids and various criminal investigations into the cult led to the practices of

"sharing" and "flirty fishing" being denounced by the cult. In 1987, it was announced that practitioners would be excommunicated. The group also decided to change its name to The Family, to distance itself from the more outrageous occurrences in the past.

Berg died in 1994 aged 75, while living in virtual exile. The Family released a charter in 1995, and now looks to Maria as the head of its organization. They tend to live quite self-sufficiently in small communes that are scattered throughout the world, and there are an estimated 9,000 full-time members (Family figures). In the USA, UK, and other European countries, Family members have been investigated by government agencies, but despite this, today's Family seems very far removed from Berg's extremist views and practices.

Chapter Five

SINISTER SECTS

MAGIC AND MURDER

THE SECTS AND CULTS WHICH HAVE ATTRACTED the most interest through the ages are those that have central beliefs which the majority of us would describe as "evil." Although sects which believe murder is justified are not necessarily followers of Black Magic, and vice versa, both types of beliefs have a basic psychological similarity. Followers believe that by carrying out certain actions that are essentially "bad," they are in effect guaranteeing their own salvation.

Satanists such as Aleister Crowley advocated the denial of the traditional moral code. It was good to commit adultery, to lie, to steal—indeed, it was important that the soul was satisfied in whatever it desired. It was beliefs like these that led such cults to be linked with strange sexual orgies and blood sacrifices. Under the instruction of their Grand Masters, followers of Satanism would become obsessed with selling their souls to the Devil.

Equally disturbing are a group of cult leaders whose personalities have persuaded others to commit murder in the name of their beliefs. The most infamous of these eerie egomaniacs is the man with the swastika carved on his forehead—Charles Manson. Serving nine life sentences, Manson remains unrepentant for instructing his followers to commit numerous murders.

Other cults have specifically targeted their victims on racial grounds. Nation of Yahweh was a black supremacist organization whose initiation rites allegedly included "smoking" a white man. The activities of the Ku Klux Klan have caused even more terror among the USA's black population.

Although the activities of these cults can be extremely frightening, it is worth noting that they only receive so much publicity because they are extreme. These power-crazed leaders operate at the very edge of society, spreading a dangerous philosophy that, thankfully, the majority of us choose to ignore.

A Grand Wizard in ceremonial purple and a state leader dressed in green stand before a burning cross. The KKK insists the cross is a Christian symbol, but the group's dark history doesn't lend credence to their claim.

CHARLES MANSON AND THE FAMILY

***P**olice officers remove the bodies of Sharon Tate and her friends from the Cielo Drive home of film director Roman Polanski.*

In August 1969, Hollywood reeled at the news of a massacre at the home of famous film director Roman Polanski. His beautiful wife, actress Sharon Tate, was found with a makeshift noose around her neck, and her back and chest were covered in 16 stab wounds. She was eight months pregnant at the time of her death.

Four guests at the massive Los Angeles house were also the victims of what looked to police like a frenzied attack. Steven Parent, aged 18, was the first to be killed. He was shot four times at close range, and stabbed once as he tried to drive away from the ranch in his car. Abigail Folger and her financier boyfriend Voytek Frykowski were found dead on the back lawn. Both had been stabbed as they tried to flee—Frykowski a horrific 51 times. He had also been shot twice and battered around the head. The words "political piggy" and "pig" had been daubed in blood on the walls along with what looked like a Black Panther gang sign. Sharon Tate's

body was found tied by the neck to that of Hollywood hairdresser Jay Seebrig. Seebrig had also bled to death from savage multiple stab wounds.

The scene at the mansion was the most depraved murder most of the officers involved had ever had to cover, and this led to a series of mistakes in the way evidence was collected over the following few days. In the end, the wiping of fingerprints, lack of communication between police departments and the bizarre overlooking of key evidence all contributed to the exceptional year-and-a-half it took to arrest and convict Charles Manson.

Manson is one of recent history's most infamous figures. He portrayed himself at his trial as a victim of society, and told Judge Charles Order that he was simply reflecting what the establishment had done to him. He still maintains he is innocent, and despite serving nine life

MANSON'S FORMATIVE YEARS

Born in 1934 on November 11 or 12 (his mother could never remember which), Charles Milles Manson had a far from normal upbringing. After being deserted by the father of her baby, 16-year-old Kathleen Maddox found it hard to cope with a child, and often left the young boy with her family or friends while she took off, funding her adventures with petty crime. When the police caught up with her and her brother after they had robbed a gas station, she left Manson with her fundamentalist parents while she served three years in jail.

The nine-year-old boy was finally collected by his errant mother when she gained parole, and the two took off, exploring the East Coast. For a while Manson regained some stability, but Kathleen fell in love with a man who didn't want someone else's child around. When he was finally abandoned at a home for boys in Indiana, Manson began his long criminal education. By the time he was released into his aunt and uncle's care when he was 20, he had been in and out of boys' homes and reformation institutions for over ten years. He also had a long history of petty crime.

Manson was married briefly in 1955 to a young woman called Rosalie, and had a son whom they called Charlie, after his father. But life quickly went off the rails again, and when he was jailed for a further five years, Rosalie left him, taking the young Charlie with her. She later filed for divorce.

At the age of 32, Manson walked out of Terminal Island Penitentiary after a ten-year sentence for, among other things, pimping. It was March 21, 1967, and this angry young man from Kentucky walked out of the prison into an atmosphere of anti-establishmentarianism and free love. Within two years, he would become the beloved guru of his Family members.

89

An informal snapshot of Charles Manson with his makeshift Family.

THE WORDS "POLITICAL PIGGY" AND "PIG" HAD BEEN DAUBED IN BLOOD ON THE WALLS

sentences with no hope of ever being released, he also attends his parole hearings, and has never shown any remorse. The self-proclaimed prophet has made so many rambling statements since his conviction that it is difficult to extract the facts. Indeed, if it wasn't for Linda Kasabian, who turned state's evidence in return for immunity from seven murder charges, the truth about the Manson's Family might never have surfaced.

After leaving prison in 1967, Manson drifted to San Francisco, where he collected together the core of what would become The Family. Young women seemed particularly attracted to Manson, and soon he was traveling around the West Coast with a busload of women, all of whom had sex with him on a regular basis. Sex was central to The Family way of life, as was the use of LSD and other hallucinatory drugs. At the trial, Linda Kasabian told the jury how Manson would

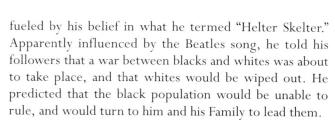

Left: Susan Atkins, Linda Kasabian, and Leslie Van Houten present an image of middle class respectability at their trial.

Right: Family members shaved their heads during the trial in support of Manson (below).

organize group orgies between Family members, which escalated to the point where he told "everybody to make love to everybody … and it didn't matter who was laying beside you, man or woman. You touched and made love to everyone."

By 1969, The Family settled at the Spahn Movie Ranch, famously giving its owner a Beach Boys gold disk in payment. Manson had met Dennis Wilson, a member of the famous band, when he was desperately trying to forge a career as a pop star himself. It was alleged at the trial that part of Manson's motive against the people he ordered to be killed was that they were successful in Hollywood circles, whereas his musical ability had been largely ignored.

The ranch became home to more than fifty people at its height, but was mostly populated by the core Family members. These were people like Susan Atkins, a teenage dropout; Leslie Van Houten, a model student who went off the rails after her parents divorced; Bobby Beausoleil, the handsome actor who had links with Satanic cults; and the wealthy Sandra Good, who still campaigns for Manson's release from jail on the grounds he had an unfair trial. Many other people drifted in and out of the commune. At one point, Manson was keen to attract bikers to the ranch, allegedly for protection. He used the women as bait, asking them to make the menacing gang members more than welcome.

Manson's paranoia about attack from outsiders was fueled by his belief in what he termed "Helter Skelter." Apparently influenced by the Beatles song, he told his followers that a war between blacks and whites was about to take place, and that whites would be wiped out. He predicted that the black population would be unable to rule, and would turn to him and his Family to lead them.

Various testimonies from ex-members have alleged that Manson was an admirer of Hitler, and this seems to be backed up by Manson's bizarre act of carving a swastika on his forehead during his trial. Linda Kasabian also testified that Manson told the group that the ranch was being watched by black militant groups which knew that Manson was aware of their plans for a race war. His paranoia grew to the point where the ranch was guarded day and night, and the bikers became frequent guests.

On August 8, 1969, Manson decided it was time for "Helter Skelter" and that he would initiate the war. It was with this aim in mind that he sent Tex Watson, Susan

BY THE
TIME THE
FAMILY
MEMBERS
HAD
FINISHED,
THE COUPLE
HAD BEEN
STABBED
87 TIMES

Atkins, Linda Kasabian, and Patricia Krenwinkel (Katie) to 10050 Cielo Drive, the home of Roman Polanski and Sharon Tate. What happened that night is legendary, but the messages daubed on the walls were supposed to lead police to the obvious conclusion, that this was a race-related killing.

The following night, seven Family members, including Manson, broke into the home of supermarket president Leno LaBianca and his wife, Rosemary. Why they were chosen as "Helter Skelter" victims isn't known, but this time Manson entered the house along with his team of assassins. It was the same group as the night before, only this time Leslie Van Houten and Clem Grogan also joined in. Manson left the house after stealing the couple's wallets and helping tie them up. By the time The Family members had finished, the couple had been stabbed 87 times. Mr LaBianca was left with the word "war" carved on his front and a carving fork stuck in his stomach. Mrs LaBianca was held face down on her bed and stabbed 41 times. Phrases such as "Death to Pigs" were daubed over the walls of the house, and "Healter Skelter" (sic) was written in blood on the fridge door. The group of murderers ate the LaBiancas' food before they eventually left.

Manson had managed the ultimate manipulation. His followers loved him so much they would kill for him.

TRIAL AND ERROR

Manson's strongest supporters, including one-time Family member Sandra Good, claim that Manson's trial and subsequent sentencing were a farce, whipped up by the media frenzy. Manson was denied the right to represent himself, and he spent much of the trial watching the prosecution from a prison room on a television screen. When he was allowed in court, he tended to interrupt proceedings with bizarre behavior such as arriving with his head shaved or instructing his fellow female defendants not to testify. On one occasion, he jumped over the witness box and threatened to attack the judge. Security was tightened as Family members on the outside issued death threats, and Leslie Van Houten's lawyer disappeared (his body was found two months after the trial ended).

It took a quarter of an hour for the clerk to read out the verdicts on the 27 counts with which the four defendants were charged. Manson, despite not actually carrying out the Tate–LaBianca murders, was found guilty on seven counts of first degree murder because he had instructed the other Family members to kill for him. Patricia Krenwinkel and Susan Atkins received the same sentence, and Leslie Van Houten was found guilty on two counts of murder—the LaBianca deaths.

All received the death penalty, but Californian law was changed the following year, and all the sentences were commuted to life imprisonment.

All the defendants are in theory eligible for parole, but only Leslie Van Houten has any real chance of seeing the outside world again. In a rare interview published in *The Washington Post* on August 7, 1994, she spoke of her remorse, and how the whole group had been taken in by Manson's re-education program.

Manson himself makes the most of his parole hearings, most probably because they are televised. At the last parole hearing, on March 27, 1997, Manson still showed no sign of repentance, and challenged the judges to see him as a victim of society. The board took only 20 minutes to decide that Manson "would pose an unreasonable risk and danger to society and a threat to public safety if released" before they sent him back to his cell.

*E*rvil LeBaron set up his cult church in the self-named Colonia LeBaron
in Mexico, where his activities weren't as closely monitored by the law.

CHURCH *of* THE LAMB *of* GOD

Since the US government passed the Edmunds Law outlawing polygamy in 1822, Mormons have faced a very real problem with some of their religious doctrines. Their founder and his successor, both of whom are treated as prophets, advocated plural marriage, insisting: "the only men who become gods are those who enter into polygamy." By the end of the 1800s, the government responded to the growing numbers of polygamous Mormon families with the Edmunds-Tucker Act. The Church of Jesus Christ of Latter-Day Saints decided to denounce polygamy, and made it known that practitioners would be excommunicated.

This radical about-face of one of the religion's basic principles led to many splinter groups forming, most of which were keen to continue the polygamous way of life. The majority of these communities re-established themselves either in Mexico or close to the border,

because the law there is more relaxed in relation to family set-up. It is important to note that the mainstream Mormon Church actively seeks to disassociate itself from these Mormon fundamentalist groups.

Joel LeBaron formed the Church of the First Born of the Fullness of Time in 1955, allegedly after a visit from two heavenly messengers who told him he was the chosen one. Joel came from a strong Mormon fundamentalist background, and at some point in their lives each of his four brothers set up their own Church. One of his brothers, Ervil LeBaron, became Joel's right-hand man in the Church of the First Born until quarrels about basic principles forced Joel to excommunicate Ervil in 1971.

Ervil LeBaron formed the Church of the Lamb of God, a very extreme cult that would ultimately claim over twenty lives. Ervil believed passionately in the doctrine advocated by Mormon prophet Brigham Young—blood atonement. In effect, this means that sometimes the fact that Christ spilt his blood for us is not enough; a true believer may have to spill the blood of the sinner to save his soul. The killing is justified because the sinner will have paid for his crime in the appropriate manner.

Members of the radical sect worshiped Ervil as God's representative on earth. Consequently, the community of followers, now based in Mexico's Baja California, believed that what Ervil preached was directly from the mouth of God. His sermons were passionate, especially about defectors from the cult, whom he said had to be killed to save their souls. A

JOEL WAS BEATEN AND THEN SHOT. THE MURDER FULFILLED ERVIL'S PROPHECY

lawyer later refered to this leader, saying "this brainwashing, this indoctrination, the type of mind games that he perpetrated on the family is unforgivable."

Ervil is believed to have been responsible for ordering the deaths of over two dozen people. His first was the self-serving murder of his brother and rival, Joel. Ervil had predicted the death of the leader of the Church of the First Born because he was "a false prophet." On August 20, 1972, Joel was beaten and then shot and killed. The gruesome murder fulfilled Ervil's prophecy. Over the following nine years, many more murders took place, including one of Ervil's own wives (he had 13), his pregnant daughter, rival cult members, and defectors. At one point, under his orders, an armed group of his followers attacked the nearby community of his dead brother's Church. In December 1974, the group sneaked into the rival compound at night and set fire to one of the houses. When the alarm was raised and followers rushed out to see what was happening, Ervil's assassins opened fire with semi-automatic weapons. A journalist reporting at the time called it "a miracle" that only two people died.

In 1980, Ervil LeBaron was convicted of murder. He received a sentence of life imprisonment. On August 16, 1981, he had a heart attack, and died in jail. However, the death of the fanatical Ervil was not the end of his band of fundamentalist followers. One of his 54 children, Aaron, took over as the "Great Grand Patriarch."

According to journalists Jack Anderson and Jan Moller, who have researched the cult, Aaron tried to bind together the dwindling numbers of his father's Church though a mixture of intimidation and money. He was also

THE BOOK OF THE LAMB OF GOD

Before he died in prison, Ervil LeBaron completed a 510-page manuscript on the teachings of the Church of the Lamb of God. He outlined how the members of his Church would rise up to take over the world, and how deserters were "sons of perdition" who must be killed before the Kingdom of God could advance.

There are allegedly a total of 15 paragraphs in the text that directly refer to the three men who were killed for leaving the group in 1988. It is also possible that Ervil left further orders with his followers, in what must be one of the most bizarre cases of murder by proxy ever seen.

a firm believer in the basic principles of the Church—polygamy and blood atonement included.

On June 27, 1988, three former members were shot dead within minutes of each other. Even more tragically, one of the victims had his 8-year-old daughter with him. As Duane Chynoweth was shot, the girl screamed, alerting the killers to the fact she had witnessed the murder. She was shot twice in the face, and died.

Aaron LeBaron was sentenced to 45 years in prison for ordering the killings. Several other cult members were also given custodial sentences, but Jacqueline LeBaron, Aaron's sister and a powerful figure in the group, had gone into hiding by the time of the trial. The prosecution vowed to find her and bring her to justice.

NATION OF YAHWEH

In what seems to be an extreme case of power spiraling out of control, the Nation of Yahweh cult, based in Miami, started life as a pro-education movement, and ended up being a fanatical, murderous society in search of world domination.

The cult's leader, Yahweh Ben Yahweh (Hebrew for "God, Son of God"), is currently serving an 18-year prison sentence in Lewisburg Penitentiary. He was charged under the crime of RICO (Racketeering-Influenced Corrupt Organizations). The 1992 trial linked him and six other Nation of Yahweh members with, among other crimes, arson, extortion, and murder.

Yahweh moved to Florida in 1979 with Linda Gaines. Together they established a group that would be known variously as the "Yahwehs" or "Black Hebrew Israelites." Their supporters quickly grew, and Yahweh was applauded by local officials for bringing a sense of purpose to poorer districts. He was allegedly awarded millions of dollars of tax breaks, and even had a day of honor named after him by Miami's mayor.

On the face of it, Yahweh's Temple of Love building, which he bought in 1980, was the center of various businesses, including a food store and printing shop. Yahweh Ben Yahweh preached that black people are the real Jews, and that God and Jesus are also black. Blacks were finally going to inherit the earth after years of oppression. His teachings were popular, and membership increased rapidly. It isn't known how many members the Nation of Yahweh encompasses, but their own literature says it has members in 1,300 US cities and has even forged enclaves of believers in other parts of the world.

In 1982, the organization took a profound change of direction when Yahweh began preaching much more fanatically. He insisted followers believe he was the Son of God, that blacks would rise up and kill the "white devils" in a race war, and that members must obey his every word.

As the cult's doctrines took on a more sinister flavor, secrecy surrounding the organization was increased to the point of paranoia. The Temple of Love was guarded by specially chosen armed members called the "Circle of Ten." Anyone who wanted to visit the temple was searched by these armed bodyguards.

It is unlikely that many facts about Yahweh Ben Yahweh would have ever been made public, despite the fact the FBI stated at the trial that they had been keeping the cult under surveillance for nearly ten years, if it hadn't been for one man. Robert Rozier, an important member of the Nation of Yahweh, became the prosecution's star witness, and gave the court a detailed description of what went on behind the guarded doors of the temple. In return, he "was rewarded with a reduced sentence after pleading guilty to killing four people," according to the Abraham Foundation Inc., a pro-Yahweh organization.

Through Rozier, the court heard how members had to pledge total obedience to Yahweh, abandon their normal clothes and adopt white robes and turbans, give their money to the organization, and abandon their outside families. Their lives became totally regulated by the man they thought was the Son of God. He even told them when they could sleep.

Absolute loyalty to Yahweh meant making the ultimate sacrifice. Nation of Yahweh followers had to be prepared not only to die for their guru, but to kill for him as well. Yahweh Ben Yahweh's inner circle knew all too well what these promises meant. According to Rozier, Yahweh Ben Yahweh formed a secretive "Brotherhood" within the cult, and its members carried out their guru's wishes without question. The price for becoming a "Brother," one of Yahweh Ben Yahweh's chosen few, was killing a "white devil" and bringing back proof in the form of a body part.

According to the "background facts" presented at the

Yahweh Ben Yahweh, once honored for his good works by Miami's mayor, is now serving an 18-year prison sentence for arson, extortion, and murder.

YAHWEH'S DEATH ANGELS

The 1996 appeal hearing of Yahweh Ben Yahweh and six of his followers took place on January 5 before the United States Court of Appeal. All points of the appeal were rejected, and the seven members of the Nation of Yahweh were returned to jail.

During the appeal, a summary of the crimes was presented to the judges. It detailed the murders and other acts of brutality commited, according to the court, under the orders of Yahweh Ben Yahweh.

These extraordinary crimes were carried out against people trying to leave the cult, random "white devils," and people Yahweh Ben Yahweh felt were in competition with his growing empire of businesses.

Aston Green decided he wanted to leave the cult, but went to the temple building before trying to make his escape, to pick up his Bible. He was beaten to the point of death by a group of about ten cult members before being taken to some wasteland and beheaded. According to court testimonies, Yahweh Ben Yahweh was delighted.

Random killings also took place to earn the Brothers a place in the elite inner circle. Clair Walters was found in a hotel with an ear missing and his throat cut. Rozier testified that cult member Ardmore Canton had showed him the left ear of the murdered white man.

At least two other members told Rozier that they had killed white men in accordance with their leader's wishes, but the prosecution's star witness was no angel himself. It is thought he carried out at least four murders during his time as a member of the gang.

Right: Yahweh and Xavier Suarez at the opening of the First Rate Food store in 1990.

Below: Other Yahweh businesses included a resort hotel on Biscayne Boulevard.

95

THE TEMPLE OF LOVE WAS GUARDED BY THE ARMED "CIRCLE OF TEN"

1996 appeal, the self-proclaimed Son of God was by now teaching followers that one day "his group would chase white men, whom he referred to as 'white devils,' from the face of the earth by killing them." Those who put an end to the white race would be his "death angels."

It isn't definitely known whether the Nation of Yahweh continues to operate on the same level, and it should be made clear that there were many members who never believed in Yahweh Ben Yahweh's commitment to eradicating the white man through murder. However, as with many underground groups, there are supporters of the leader on the Internet. One specific page, "The Universe of Yahweh," gives a comprehensive comparison between the fanatical, dangerous leader and Jesus Christ.

SATANISM

There is little, or even no evidence for the existence of the devil-worshiping, child-abusing Satanic sects that have infiltrated the public consciousness in the past few years. Despite many scare stories, the most widely publicized of which was probably the Orkney Island case in the UK, recent research on both sides of the Atlantic has claimed that our ideas of well-organized groups of Satanists are actually a myth.

Satanism or devil-worship does exist, but has been subject to many misnomers. When the majority of us hear of Satanists, it is generally via the media, and usually when a murderer goes public and blames his or her crime on some kind of pact with the Devil. This type of "Satanist" has all the credibility of teenagers who dabble with the Ouija board, or rock groups who package their act with so-called "Satanist"

*T*he different faces of Aleister Crowley, who often enjoyed posing in his self-appointed role as Magician and Satanist.

paraphernalia. A true practicing Satanist would also dismiss these people as having nothing to do with what they worship. A Satanist doesn't approve of ritual killings, because human life is ultimately sacred.

Allegedly labeled the "Great Beast" from the Bible's Book of Revelation by his mother, a devout member of the pious Plymouth Brethren, Aleister Crowley (1875–1947) is often credited with the beginnings of modern Satanism. In reality, the worship of natural human desires personified by Satan dates much further back, but there is no denying that Crowley instigated a revival with his "Do what thou wilt shall be the whole of the law" philosophy.

Crowley became interested in the occult as a student at Cambridge University, and later became a member of the secretive occult organization the Hermetic Order of the Golden Dawn. According to his writings, Crowley had a "divine" experience while he and his wife were staying in

Egypt. Over three days, *The Book of the Law* was dictated by voices only Crowley could hear. When the experience was over, Crowley claimed he had been chosen as the prophet of a new age of "Force and Fire." At the center of the new philosophy was the adage "There is no god but man," which outraged traditional religious thinkers, but Crowley interpreted *The Book of the Law* in much the same way as modern Satanists conduct their lives—that the self was all-important. Innate human desires, particularly sexual ones, must be satisfied. A new age was to be ushered in, and conventional religions would be dissolved while what Crowley called "magick" would finally allow people to truly find themselves.

LOVEDAY DIED AT THE ABBEY; HIS WIFE CLAIMED HE HAD BEEN POISONED

While the core of Crowley's teachings doesn't sound so strange in this era of new age belief, some of his teaching methods were bizarre, and created much publicity via the newspapers of the time. Calling himself "The Great Beast 666" and filing his teeth to points didn't help his cause either, but the death of one of his followers fueled a scandal that led to him being labeled "the wickedest man in the world."

One of Crowley's favorite students was Raoul Loveday, an Oxford University graduate. Loveday died while he was staying at Crowley's Abbey of Thelema with his wife. She promptly flew back to the UK and told the press he had been poisoned by blood he had drunk in one of Crowley's ceremonies. It is now thought that Loveday drank from a contaminated water supply, but the damage was done, and Crowley's cult was expelled from Italy.

Crowley's notoriety waned, his wife became an alcoholic, and he spent much of the rest of his life traveling. He died in a far from glorious state, at 72, addicted to heroin, in a seaside hotel in Hastings, England.

Ironically, Crowley's teachings have become more popular now than they were when he was alive. His writings have been reprinted, his personally designed set of tarot cards is one of the most popular packs available, and most recently, an exhibition of his paintings was shown in the town where he died.

97

CROWLEY'S ABBEY OF THELEMA

Now almost forgotten, Aleister Crowley's old farmhouse in Sicily, Italy, still stands as an artistic testament to Crowley's teachings. In 1920, he founded a commune which he called the Abbey of Thelema and it was there that he initiated his followers into the art of "magick." Although sensational reports of what went on at the abbey have probably been exaggerated many times, there is no denying that sexual promiscuity was high on the list of activities. The remnants of Crowley's sexual magick can still be seen on the walls of the building, depicted in many lurid, probably drug-induced, pornographic paintings.

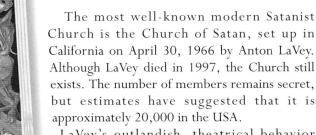

The most well-known modern Satanist Church is the Church of Satan, set up in California on April 30, 1966 by Anton LaVey. Although LaVey died in 1997, the Church still exists. The number of members remains secret, but estimates have suggested that it is approximately 20,000 in the USA.

LaVey's outlandish, theatrical behavior brought his Church to public attention with images of his rituals performed on a "living

altar" of a naked young woman. He became even more of a celebrity when he starred in Roman Polanski's film *Rosemary's Baby*, playing the Devil. It is even alleged that certain Hollywood celebrities were so taken with the High Priest that they joined the Church of Satan—Sammy Davis Jnr and Jayne Mansfield were both linked to LaVey.

Despite LaVey's shaven head, black-cloaked appearance, and all the Satanic symbolism he used, the Church of Satan philosophy is far removed from the "evil" most of us would imagine. Satanists do believe in the Devil—but not as an entity with horns and a forked tail that is idolized, but as a force of nature. The Devil is much more of a

*T*he head of the Church of Satan, Anton LaVey.

pagan concept, in essence conjured up by man and embodying the parts of human nature that the Christian Church has tried to suppress— essentially animal instincts, such as power and sexuality.

LaVey's text, *The Satanic Bible*, sets out his philosophy. Satanists are loosely tied to a central control, as it is desirable for each member to be responsible for their own actions. LaVey's nine Satanic statements are central to his brand of theology. Believing that there is no afterlife and that human life is sacred, self-indulgence is the key to Satanism. The eighth statement sums up this belief: "Satan represents all of the so-called sins, as they lead to physical or mental gratification!"

POSSESSED BY THE DEVIL?

When the press alleged the teenagers responsible for the five US Jonesboro murders in March 1988 had been involved in Satanism, no one seemed very surprised. It was the latest in a long line of inexplicable killings which the media soon aligned with devil-worship and an obsession with evil.

Brian Lane alleges in his chilling book *The Encyclopedia of Occult and Supernatural Murder* that Anton LaVey's book *The Satanic Bible* "above all others has been found in the possession of young cult killers," and suggests it is the reason most became interested in devil-worship. However, a pro-Satanist site on the Internet suggests these young killers never really read the LaVey text, as it is a complex book to digest, but they simply pick up on society's interpretation of devil-worship. Whatever the case, most of the famous "Satanic" killers were loners or members of small, self-formed groups. They had no links with the Church of Satan or other Satanic sects such as the Temple of Set, a Church of Satan offshoot.

One of the most infamous killers linked to Satanism is David Berkowitz, the "Son of Sam" murderer, who is currently

serving a sentence totaling over 300 years at the US Attica Correctional Institution. He conducted a year-long campaign during 1976–1977 when he killed six people and wounded seven more. At the time of his trial, Berkowitz told the courtroom he had made a pact with the Devil, and was told to kill his victims, mostly women, allegedly because he thought women despised him. Berkowitz shot his targets at close range, leaving little chance of survival.

Despite being convicted of all six murders, Berkowitz has often alluded to the involvement of other members of a Satanic cult allegedly called the "Twenty-two Disciples of Hell." Discrepancies in the trial evidence, particularly some of the witness descriptions of the murderer, have led to some researchers backing up the theory that more than one person was involved in the killings. Berkowitz, however, having escaped at least one attempt on his life, has now "found God," claiming in a 1997 US radio interview:"'I know that Christ has forgiven me ... I know that Satan was in me. I was demonically possessed ever since childhood. But now God has just freed me from that."

Sorcerer LaVey presides over a wedding ceremony "conceived in hell," complete with naked altar.

Satanists believe that humans are the most vicious of animals, that natural selection should also apply to the human race, where the strong have power and the weak serve them, and that all selfish needs should be satisfied. There is no heaven and there is no hell, so desires should be satisfied in this life. Sexuality is seen as one of the strongest of human desires, and the Church of Satan advocates satisfying sexual needs in any way members wish, whether it be heterosexual, homosexual, bisexual, monogamous, or involving groups. The only thing it does specify is that this satisfaction of carnal desires must be between consenting adults. This rules out sacrificing virgins and other Hollywood representations of Satanists. Yet our misconceptions about their beliefs continue.

Other surprising "rules" are that the use of drugs is not allowed, for they dull the senses of the human animal, and suicide is strongly opposed. The Black Mass, which is depicted in so many horror films, does actually take place, but is not an essential part of Satanist worship. The ritual, designed to mock the Catholic Mass, is often just a publicity stunt, and the sacrifice of both humans and animals is forbidden.

Rituals are an important part of Satanic worship, however, and LaVey was very clear on how they should be conducted. There are three types of Satanist ritual:

BELIEVING THAT THERE IS NO AFTERLIFE, SELF-INDULGENCE IS THE KEY TO SATANISM

sexual, healing, and destructive. Sexual rituals are more of a celebration of sexuality than the stereotypical orgies of fictional fame. Most followers of Satanism see monogamy as the ideal state, so the belief that sex is readily available in Satanist circles is a clear misconception. Healing ceremonies are conducted on similar principles to the Wiccan equivalent, although Satanists deny any links with their white witch counterparts because Wiccans refuse to "harm others." (The term "Wiccan" encompasses a broad spectrum of people who follow Pagan beliefs. They usually identify closely with earth magic and white witchcraft.) Satanists' destruction rituals do "curse" enemies, in an attempt to weaken their power. One of LaVey's nine Satanic principles defies the Christian doctrine of turning the other cheek, and advocates vengeance. Satanists do not, contrary to popular opinion, murder or physically harm their enemies, but they do believe in survival of the fittest and the power their self-gratification gives them.

THE KU KLUX KLAN

Six ex-Confederate soldiers in Tennessee founded the infamous brotherhood of white-robed, white-supremacist American men in 1865, following the American Civil War. According to Klan literature, their organization was born out of the harsh conditions imposed by the federal government on the Southern states, but in effect it was born from and maintained through fear.

The end of the Civil War was the end for an even greater evil—slavery. The Southern states, home to huge white-owned plantations manned by illegally transported black slaves, had lost their battle for independence from the antislavery North. Political control fell into the hands of a group known as the "Radicals" after the assassination of Abraham Lincoln by a Southern sympathizer. The Radicals, led by President Andrew Johnson, wanted to punish the slaveholders for the revolt, and employed what can be described in retrospect as a policy of occupation.

The Civil Rights Act of 1866 emancipated the slaves. Land that had once been the enforced workplace of the slaves was taken from their one-time masters and redistributed to the blacks and the poor whites. The power shift was immense. While the new government departments tried to establish a fair society for all (ironically, the men from the North, called "carpetbaggers" by their Southern counterparts, ran departments rife with

A roadside gathering of the Knights of the White Kamellia attract
passing support in suburban Texas.

GRAND WIZARDS AND CROSSWHEELS

The KKK has a definite hierarchy, even today, despite there being many factional groups. Each order looks to the Grand Wizard (or Imperial Wizard) whom they recognize as the national leader of the organization. The structure of the group is identical to how it was conceived back in 1865, but some modern factions have employed the colored robes that were adopted in the 1920s. While traditionalists wear all-white whatever their rank, Grand Wizards of the Second Era wear purple robes, their national organizers dress in red, the state leader wears green, and only regular Klansmen adopt the infamous white garb.

These outfits are generally only worn for rituals or during publicity stunts. Ironically, the Knights of the Ku Klux Klan say they don't wear the hooded robes to intimidate, but rather to maintain "anonymity in doing good works." Klansmen who adopt a regular uniform of black pants and white shirts can be recognized by the symbols on their armbands and badges.

The Crosswheel symbol is as important to the Klan as the fiery cross. It is used by all true Klan groups, and decorates their flags and literature, as well as the dubious T-shirts and trinkets that are for sale over the Internet.

The sign, which is a simple cross within a circle, is said to represent the Klan's name and have Christian and Aryan links. Although the Crosswheel was only universally adopted in the 1970s, the "blood drop" symbol has been used since the 1920s. It features a Maltese cross within a red circle, and a drop of blood in the center of the cross. According to kkk.com, an organization dedicated to keeping the history of the Ku Klux Klan alive, the blood drop "in part represents the blood of Jesus Christ, which was shed for the White Aryan Race."

ITS PRINCIPLES REMAIN THE SAME, BUT THE OBJECTS OF HATRED HAVE BROADENED

corruption), their legislation did nothing to dispel generations of bitterness and hatred.

According to the history of the Klan, as written by the Knights of the White Kamellia order of the KKK, "Blacks began flaunting their new found freedoms to the disgust of the White citizens and the terror of their wives and children. Black insolence was rampant, murders were frequent, and outrages upon women and children were beginning to be heard of."

The six men who met on Christmas Eve 1865 decided on the name "Ku Klux" from the Greek word *kyklos*, meaning "circle." Their aims were to fight for white supremacy, protect the Constitution of the United States, and maintain their rights to Christian worship.

Today, the Klan has an alarmingly prominent presence on the Internet, with many of its "branches" posting their own pages in the hope it will recruit more potential supporters. As the organization enters what it calls its "Fifth Era," its basic principles have remained the same, but the objects of hatred have broadened. Although most groups have disclaimers alleging they don't approve of illegal methods, researchers have sneered at this "acceptable" face of the Klan, and cite many examples of intimidation and worse that still go on. While some branches still operate a militant "Back to Africa" policy concerning blacks, others have started to concentrate on

101

A mob surrounds lynch victims in 1930s America. Between 1882–1951, some 3000 racially motivated deaths, mainly directed at blacks, occurred in the US.

IMPORTANT KLAN PRINCIPLES

These include "Positive Christianity"—the right of US Christian patriots to worship, especially in schools; white supremacy; the maintenance of racial differences, and opposition to all interracial marriages; upholding the original US Constitution, and always putting America first; educating against homosexuality and other "deviant" lifestyles, and closing US borders to immigration. Members must be aged over 18, white Christians, and be able to pledge allegiance to the brotherhood by agreeing to preserve the white race. Despite active persecution of Catholics in the past, some Klan orders now permit Catholic members, and women are now accepted into most "brotherhoods." Most Klan literature makes it known that it doesn't advocate violent means unless in self-defense.

homosexuals or abortion clinics as their targets.

In May 1997, 30 Klan members, all fully robed with their sinister, faceless white hoods, demonstrated outside a gay bar in Pennsylvania. The Grand Wizard who led the group at first said a prayer for the "sinners," and then went on to issue veiled threats such as: "Please don't make the next call have to be a business call."

The fear these anonymous robed fanatics instill is much the same as over a century ago. Membership has dropped dramatically since it reached its peak of about four million men in the 1920s. It is still most popular in the Southern states, but operates all over the USA, and even has an international order.

The "Fourth Era" of the Klan brought the underground organization to public attention again, particularly in the early 1980s. This was due to Klan masters appeared on television and in newspaper interviews, attempting to justify their beliefs.

Now the Klan talks about evolving into its "Fifth Era," it is an organization split by rival personalities, faction groups, and lack of money. Despite the continued insistence that they are simply protecting the interests of white Christian Americans, there is no denying the close links the KKK has with militant "white power" and neo-Nazi groups.

THERE IS NO DENYING THE CLOSE LINKS WITH "WHITE POWER" AND NEO-NAZI GROUPS

The 1990s have seen a call for the Fifth Era to emulate the traditional values of the Ku Klux Klan. Klan literature now calls for a return to secrecy, and recalls the days when faceless men rode silently through the towns of their enemies after dark. The hooded vigilantes had a strange code of practice—they would always issue a warning, often in the form of a Klan calling-card bearing the traditional blood drop symbol, and if the victim refused to leave town, then the group would return. The 1920s saw an alarming rise in intimidation, with lynching, burning of property, murders, and whippings regularly being attributed to the KKK. Prosecutions were rare, however.

According to "A Klansman's Guide to the Fifth Era," printed in an inter-Klan newsletter: "The horsemen rode with a single-minded purpose: there would be a White man's government in this country—or no government! So it will be in the Fifth Era." The same article proclaims: "No-one in the Klan movement can doubt that we are now engaged in a great war, testing whether ... the White Aryan man shall survive. As this conflict is a battle for survival, it is by definition a no-holds-barred contest." While the various leaders call for a return to the "Invisible Empire" of top-secret membership and underground combat tactics, it should be emphasized that the group has extremely limited influence, and each branch is carefully monitored by the US government.

A show of force by the Ku Klux Klan, marching in Washington DC in 1925. Such rallies were orchestrated to reinforce intimidation.

THE FIERY CROSS

The terrifying symbol of the Ku Klux Klan, the burning cross, was enough to subjugate many black people in the South even after they had been granted long overdue civil rights. KKK members believe they are upholders of the true Christian faith, believing that Eve had sexual relations with Satan, the offspring of which created the Jewish race, who then procreated with animals, producing all other nonwhite races. They use very selective quotes from the Bible to attempt to justify their "pro-white" philosophy, and also maintain that the burning cross, which is still used as part of their  initiation ceremonies, isn't blasphemous, and isn't really a "burning," but more of an "illuminating." The Klan themselves describe the symbolism as "representing the lighting of the cross, that is, the truth and the light of our sacred doctrine: the blazing spirit of Western Christian Civilization."

Despite this hard-to-rationalize "Christian" defense, there is no denying that the cross, often raised in all-black neighborhoods, was a major tool in the intimidation of KKK "enemies." The huge fires that resembled witchcraft burnings and were instigated by a group of powerful but faceless men filled with hatred reinforced the fear of the much-publicized practice of tar-and-feathering.

When the Knights of the White Kamellia was resurrected in December 1993, 40 members raised a fiery cross outside Jennings, Louisiana, and a sympathizer wrote: "one could feel the presence of the original founders among them, looking down with approval [on] an organization founded in brotherhood, for the preservation, and protection of the White race by all legal means necessary." The Knights of the White Kamellia wasted no time in emulating their forefathers, and have been linked to bomb threats, carrying arms in public, and bribing children to intimidate their Afro-American peers.

VOODOO

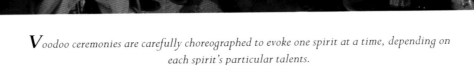

Voodoo ceremonies are carefully choreographed to evoke one spirit at a time, depending on each spirit's particular talents.

Voodoo is thought to have approximately 50 million followers world-wide. It is a diverse religion, blending African beliefs with Catholic influences, and was born out of the slave trade. Its origins are based in Haiti, where black slaves were forced to deny their own African tribal religions and adopt the Catholicism of the French plantation-owners. In practice, the Catholic saints were added to the native idols which were already worshiped.

The religion, which is much misunderstood because of fictional portrayals, is based on the belief that a group of "gods"—the loa—are in control of all things that happen. All living creatures on earth should serve the loa, who need to be "fed" to maintain their powers. Where Voodoo sits particularly uneasily with Catholicism is that the Voodoo priests will deliberately evoke these "spirits," and are often possessed by them. Most Christians believe the spirit world should not be tampered with.

Rituals involve calling on a certain loa to come down to the human world, where he or she will be asked for help. The Voodoo community, called a *société*, is headed by the houngan or mambo (priest or priestess), who can contact the loa directly. Most ceremonies are healing or love rituals, and their aim is to maintain the spiritual balance on earth. Only some deal specifically with evil, or curses. It is the use of such paraphernalia as bones, skulls, and statues which convinces outsiders that something akin to witchcraft is taking place. Each *société* has variations, such as which particular loa are venerated the most. There are some mainstream differences that have split their various adherents into separate sects. Santeria is the Cuban form of Voodoo, and also thrives in Latino areas of the USA. New Orleans Voodoo is extremely popular in the area, where they tend to perform rituals with live snakes. Other distinct forms have been identified in New York and Chicago, and Voodoo continues to thrive in Latin America and, of course, Haiti.

Voodoo shouldn't be dismissed as harmless, however. It was partially responsible for the 14 years of oppression that Haitians suffered under the tyrannical leadership of Papa Doc Duvalier. Papa Doc ruled his people through

ZOMBIFICATION

For most believers in Voodoo, the most sinister threat is the curse of zombification. It is thought that some priests possess the ultimate power—that of creating the living dead. Voodoo burials are complex affairs, with great care being taken to ensure the body cannot be raised from its coffin in a zombie state.

Haitians don't fear zombies, but are justifiably scared of being turned into one. For years, tales of zombification were dismissed despite there being many recorded cases. However, in 1937 an American ethnographer, Zora Neale Hurston, became the first Westerner to study a real-life zombie. Felicia Felix Mentor was found wandering in a semiconscious state in Haiti in 1937. Her family recognized her, despite the fact she had died and been buried 30 years earlier. Hurston's findings led to further research, most notably by Wade Davis, an American biologist who was fascinated by a 1980 account by ex-zombie Clairvius Narcisse. Narcisse had tracked down his family after recovering enough to remember who he was. He gave a detailed description of how the village boker (black magician) had poisoned him to slow his heartbeat. He said two doctors had proclaimed him dead, and despite being fully conscious, he was unable to move, and was therefore buried. The boker dug him up after the funeral, and administered another potion which let his limbs move but kept him confused. He was put to work with other zombies in a remote part of Haiti, and kept like a slave.

Davis's findings were astonishing. He effectively proved that Voodoo bokers do have the power to turn enemies into the "living dead." By administering various potions, the heart rate of the victim can be slowed to such an extent that to all intents and purposes he or she looks dead. Providing the body isn't kept underground for too long (leading to severe brain damage caused by oxygen deprivation), the boker can use further ingredients to revive the body to a satisfactorily stupor-like state. Davis identified the main ingredient of these potions as the gland secretions of a highly poisonous frog, the bouga toad, and the poison tetrodotoxin, which can be extracted from certain types of puffer fish.

Skulls and sacrificial animals are often used in Voodoo worship, as death plays an important role. The realm of the spirits is where all decisions are made.

MANY BELIEVED PAPA DOC WAS THE LOA OF DEATH, BARON SAMEDI

fear, employing black magicians as part of his entourage, and forming the dreaded Tontons Macoutes, a sinister security force. Many Haitians believed Papa Doc was the incarnation of the loa of death, Baron Samedi. Papa Doc even dressed in a black suit and wore typical Voodoo talismans to project this image.

Some even more sinister offshoots and practices have been associated with Voodoo. Some practitioners concentrate solely on worshiping the "petro loa" (the darker spirits). These groups are particularly fond of using animal sacrifices and, even more disturbing, some use human skulls and body parts in their ceremonies. One particular offshoot, which is on the very extreme edge of Voodoo worship, is the Cochon Gris. It is an intensely secretive society, and is rumored to practice cannibalism.

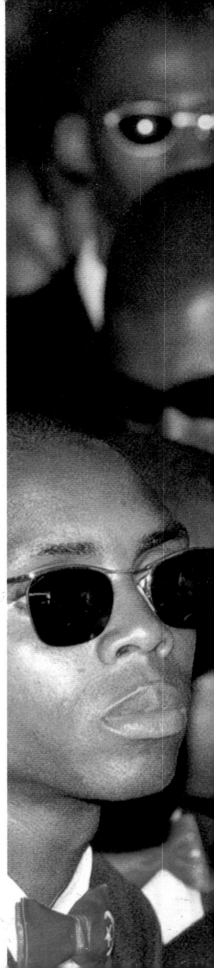

Chapter Six

MODERN MILITANTS

FIGHTING FOR BELIEFS

SOME FORM OF ANTIGOVERNMENT ACTIVITY is inevitable, if not essential to the functioning of a democracy. Free speech, freedom to form opposition groups, and freedom to criticize government policy are all valued rights that most in the Western world now cherish. But under the wide definition of "democracy," when does the importance of an individual's civil rights cross the line to become against the national interest, and when does "firm" government policy become dictatorial?

In the USA in particular, the lines are being quickly drawn. Since the Oklahoma City bombing in 1995, US government agencies have uncovered a greater threat to the American way of life than the majority of Americans ever dreamed existed. Much closer to home than the threat of Middle Eastern reprisals or South American socialism is a growing group of disaffected Americans who feel they've been let down by their countrymen.

The increase in Militia and hate groups in the US over the last twenty years has been astonishing. The FBI now deals with over 900 acts of domestic terrorism every year. Peaceful demonstration seems to be taking a back seat, as extremists and racists bond together against what they believe is a corrupt government system, to demand a "New World Order."

Bound by frustration and hatred, fueled by events such as the Branch Davidian siege and various confrontations between police and patriots—like the Ruby Ridge stand-off—and united by the technology of video, shortwave radio, and most importantly, the censorship-free Internet, a growing number of ordinary American people are finding comfort in belonging to a group of like-minded individuals, usually led by a persuasive leader. How far they will go is dependent on the individuals, but when one man, Timothy McVeigh, can take his right-wing ideology so far that he kills 168 people, it is time to ask some questions.

The Nation of Islam, the largest black power group in the US, has been accused of advocating a separatist political agenda, just like the far-right white power groups.

106

THE OKLAHOMA CITY BOMBING

On April 19, 1995, 9:02 a.m., an enormous blast ripped through the Alfred P. Murrah Federal Building in Oklahoma City. In all, 168 people died in the explosion, which wrecked the nine-storey government building. One of the main areas to feel the full force of the blast was the daycare center for under-fives, situated on the second floor, where 15 of the 21 children died. America was in shock.

Twenty-five months later, a federal jury returned 11 guilty verdicts on Timothy McVeigh, a 29-year-old Gulf War veteran, who, according to the prosecution, had become obsessed with survivalist and Patriot politics.

It was first suspected that the bombing had been carried out by international terrorists, but when the authorities investigated the scene, they followed a trail from the truck which had been parked outside the building to a rental firm called Elliot's Body Shop in Kansas. The employee who had signed over the vehicle supplied the police with enough details for a composite drawing to be created. Three witnesses who had been

McVeigh HAS BEEN SENTENCED TO DIE FROM LETHAL INJECTION

near the building identified the man in the drawing as someone they'd seen loitering outside the Alfred P. Murrah Building at approximately 8:40 a.m.

Almost simultaneously, checks with local motels led to the suspect being identified as a Timothy J. McVeigh, and an ex-colleague of McVeigh's contacted the FBI, saying he'd recognized him in the composite drawings, and warned, according to the criminal complaint filed against McVeigh, that he was known to hold "extreme rightwing views."

As it turned out, McVeigh was already under arrest. He had been stopped an hour and a half after the explosion, approximately one-and-a-half hours' drive from the city center. His car had no license plates, and he was in possession of a weapon. Forensics later revealed he had residue from explosives on his clothes.

McVeigh was very quickly linked to brothers James and Terry Nichols, and all three were subsequently questioned about the bombing. Terry Nichols was

The north side of the Alfred P. Murrah building lies in ruins following the explosion of a home-made bomb.

POLITICS OF HATE

McVeigh leaves court on April 21, 1995, surrounded by law enforcement officials. He has refused to give investigators any further information about the bombing, so the search for co-conspirators has come to an end.

Timothy McVeigh was fascinated with guns. He allegedly only joined the army so he could carry an M-16. He was also a keen survivalist, had purchased land to practice shooting, and kept a stockpile of food and ammunition in case of nuclear attack. Other "clues" came out during his questioning. One was his fascination with a book called *The Turner Diaries*—a fictional account of a race war in America that features the blowing up of FBI headquarters; the book is considered essential reading by most white supremacist and race-hate groups.

McVeigh was also deeply disturbed by the siege at Waco. He considered the whole fiasco to have been orchestrated by the authorities, and that the eighty or so dead were practically martyrs for the Patriot cause. He had made no secret of his feelings, writing angry letters to local papers, and telling friends that the government would never win a war against its own people.

believed to have helped McVeigh build the truck bomb.

Both McVeigh and Terry Nichols were found guilty. James was later released without being charged. McVeigh has been sentenced to die by lethal injection, while Nichols, who didn't actually plant the bomb, is serving life with no hope of parole. A third man, Michael Fortier, also knew about the plot, but provided evidence for the prosecution, so he received a lighter sentence.

Although America generally breathed a collective sigh of relief when the cases were over, with President Clinton calling the end of the trial "a long overdue day," some commentators were still uneasy about certain facts.

There were bound to be the usual conspiracy theories expounded by the far right, that the whole thing had been masterminded by Clinton's federal government, or even higher up, by the sinister "Socialist New World Order," which desperately wanted to discredit the activities of the Patriot movement.

Many people believe more than one co-conspirator is hiding in the shadowy underworld of the Militia and hate groups. They find it hard to believe that two men could, on their own, construct a 4,000 lb bomb, even if they had been in the army together. It would have taken an extraordinary amount of organizing, covert buying of materials, and surveillance work. Anyway, say the unofficial investigators, there are all sorts of coincidences that link the men—McVeigh in particular—to groups which have been labeled "domestic terrorists."

McVeigh is thought to have had links with the Michigan Militia and a group of Christian Identity followers (extremist, rightwing, racist, so-called "Christian" groups which believe only white people are the chosen children of God). One other link that shouldn't be overlooked is McVeigh's obsession with a particular date—April 19 is a special day for Patriots, as it saw the execution of one of the movement's more infamous members, Richard Snell, and on the anniversary, McVeigh planted his bomb. Snell had murdered a black police officer, and was a member of the Christian Identity group, The Covenant, the Sword and the Arm of the Lord. The date is also significant because in 1775 it saw the start of the American Revolution, and it is also the day the Branch Davidian compound was raided.

Despite all the unanswered questions, neither Nichols nor McVeigh suggested anyone else was involved in the plot, and both refused to give any further evidence. McVeigh is in the process of appealing his death sentence.

POSSE COMITATUS

*T*he Posse has set up its own "townships" in an attempt to bypass the restrictions of the law.

The Posse Comitatus is typical of the far-right, extremist, armed groups that are on the increase in the USA. It is also one of the older, more well-established groups, and has close ties to the supposedly religious Christian Identity movement. Its symbol is a man hanging from a noose, tied to a tree, with the words "It's time for old-fashioned American justice."

The group name loosely translates as "power to the county," which is the basis of all their beliefs. Members refuse to accept any authority higher than a county sheriff, believing the federal government is a corrupt organization dedicated to taking away the rights of the true American citizen. They also hold the racist belief that the federal government, all banking institutions, and officers of the state from the FBI to the police are controlled by the Jewish community, who are trying to deprive white Americans of their right to sovereignty.

Mike Beach formed the group in 1969, in Oregon. Beach has been closely linked to the neo-Nazi group the Silver Shirts, a group of pro-Hitler sympathizers. It initially appealed to farmers who, despite struggling for years on unproductive land, were having loans recalled by the banks, and were therefore losing not only their livelihoods, but their homes. Anger and bitterness are essential for the survival of these hate groups, and Beach's Posse Comitatus gave these negative feelings a focus.

Although many people identify themselves with the Posse, it isn't a close-knit organization; rather, it contains smaller factions who are bound together with common goals and by the literature the group produces. The innocuously titled Family Farm Preservation Group is only one of these splinter groups. The organization as a whole also identifies with other Militia, pro-white and neo-Nazi organizations, attending rallies and sharing magazines and so-called "intelligence," although all of these groups have their own brand of antifederalism.

The Posse Comitatus advocates distancing oneself from the "tyranny" of the state, and members prepare for the eventual day when they will have to fight for their rights in a conflict equaling that of the American Civil War. To retain their individual freedom, Posse members don't pay taxes, don't register for automobile licenses or marriage certificates, or send their children to state-run schools. The ideal is to raise a generation of children who officially don't exist, and are therefore ultimately "free." If this

MURDERER OR MARTYR?

George W. Kahl is considered a hero, not only by the Posse Comitatus, but by other so-called Patriot organizations such as the Aryan Nations and the NAAWP (National Association for the Advancement of White People). Kenneth S. Stern, in his book *A Force Upon the Plain*, describes Kahl as a man who was "a member of the Posse Comitatus ... he was also a tax protester, wore a miniature hangman's noose on his lapel and had been convicted of tax evasion in 1977."

When Kahl was released from jail, he continued to avoid paying taxes and violated his parole. In a confrontation with police on February 13, 1993, in North Dakota, Kahl made it through a roadblock after two marshals had been shot dead and four other people had been wounded. Three were police, and one was Kahl's 20-year-old son, who had been traveling with Kahl in the automobile. Kahl went on the run, but was tracked down to a small farmhouse in Imboden, Arkansas. On June 3, he was surrounded by almost a hundred armed officers. There was a massive exchange of fire (Kahl is thought to have had over 100,000 rounds of ammunition) which left both a sheriff and Kahl dead. The farmhouse exploded in flames. Subsequently, over two hundred people attended George W. Kahl's funeral.

*A*ugust Kreis, a Christian Identity leader with close ties to the Posse Comitatus, preaches with his gun and Bible present.

MEMBERS DON'T PAY TAXES OR REGISTER FOR LICENSES

were the sum total of Posse misdemeanors, then it is doubtful whether the group would have hit the headlines, but in common with other Patriot groups, the Posse is extremely well armed. It runs training camps for its members, teaching hand-to-hand combat, bomb-making skills, and murder using poison. It also urges members to arm themselves and their families, making sure a stockpile of weapons and provisions is kept in preparation for the day when true Americans are rallied to take on their "enemies."

Even stranger, Posse members don't like dealing with legal currency. More than one member has been charged with distributing huge amounts of forged notes, but in their warped view of society, they see the monetary system as being controlled by the "Jewish nation," and therefore feel justified in sabotaging the establishment. They favor a barter system, although some members don't seem to have a problem with stealing, and collect funds in the form of gold, silver, and precious stones.

Terry Nichols, the man who stood trial for allegedly helping Timothy McVeigh construct the 4,000-lb Oklahoma City bomb, had close ties with the Posse Comitatus, and was one of its more extreme members. He refused to put license plates on his truck, and threw away his voting card and passport. He wrote to local authorities, declaring he was no longer a citizen of their corrupt state. He met McVeigh while they were in the army, and after the two had left, formed a small cell of Patriots. After a string of court cases against Nichols on charges of debt, it is alleged that the two friends decided it was time to face the authorities head-on.

ARMY OF GOD

"**A**nnihilating abortuaries is the purest form of worship," claims Freedom Fox, the bizarrely named leader of the Army of God. The group, which has claimed responsibility for a series of bombings in the USA over the past few years, is highly secretive, and may not even be an organized, cohesive group, according to some current affairs commentators.

On January 29, 1998, a home-made bomb placed on a walkway outside the building ripped holes in the Alabama New Woman, All Women Health Care Clinic. The clinic, as well as being responsible for general women's health, carried out abortions. A police officer, Robert D. Sanderson, who was working off-duty as a security guard, was the first person in the country to be killed by a bomb at an abortion clinic, but the sixth to die at the hands of anti-abortion campaigners. A senior nurse, Emily Lyons, was injured in the blast and eventually lost an eye.

Letters to various newspapers, allegedly from the Army of God, claimed responsibility for the nail-filled bomb, but the FBI already had their sights on one man.

On May 5, 1998, the FBI upped their reward from $100,000 to $1 million for information leading to the arrest of Eric Robert Rudolph. Rudolph's truck was seen by witnesses at the scene of the bombing, and shortly afterwards a man wearing a wig was seen driving off at speed. The truck was found abandoned, and Rudolph had disappeared. There is talk that someone is protecting Rudolph, especially considering he is on the FBI's most wanted list, his photograph has been circulated on television and the Internet, and all leads in his native town in Macon County, North Carolina, have been exhausted. The FBI believe he is connected to the Army of God.

Other acts of home-grown terrorism linked to the group have included the fire-bombing of two abortion clinics in Florida in May 1982; the kidnapping of Dr Hector Zevallos, who performed abortions, and his wife, in August of the same year; the murder of Dr David Gunn in 1993; a bomb blast at a popular gay night-club in Georgia in February 1997; and various other extremist acts of violence. Bomb-making details in the Army of God letters led police to believe they were dealing with a well-organized group.

A man called Don Ben Anderson was found guilty of kidnapping Dr Zevallos, and told police that he was a member of the Army of God. It was the first the press and the police had heard of the movement, but it wasn't to be the last.

When Rachelle Shannon was arrested for the 1993 wounding of Dr George Tiller in Kansas, she was found to be the owner of a curious, spiral-bound, 70-page booklet entitled "When Life Hurts, We Can Help—THE ARMY OF GOD." The document was buried in her garden. It explained to police

***H**andwritten letters claimed responsibility for bombing the Alabama clinic.*

CENTENNIAL OLYMPIC PARK BOMBING

At 1:20 a.m. on Saturday July 27, 1996, a 40-lb bomb exploded in Centennial Olympic Park, in Atlanta, Georgia. The Summer Olympics were being held in the city at the time, so the park was busy with people, and the incident made international news headlines. When the bomb exploded, it killed one person and injured over a hundred. It was a particularly vicious device, as it contained a large amount of masonry nails, which were thrown out with great force when it exploded. The FBI have discovered links between the structure of the bomb and those constructed by the so-called Army of God followers. They want to question Eric Robert Rudolph, the same man allegedly seen fleeing the site of the Birmingham, Alabama, bombing, although the Army of God haven't claimed responsibility for the Olympic Park atrocity as yet.

One of the FBI's most wanted, fugitive Eric Robert Rudolph may have links to the Army of God bombings.

why Shannon had shot the doctor in both his arms.

The booklet, produced by the person or organization calling themselves the Army of God, details "99 covert ways to stop abortion." Its cover shows a picture of a small girl cuddling a doll, but its content is much more shocking. It gives detailed information on how to make and plant a bomb, how to purchase and disseminate biological weapons, and how to construct timing devices.

An interview with the organization's supposed leader,

"EVERY PRO-LIFE PERSON SHOULD COMMIT TO DISARMING AT LEAST ONE BABY KILLER"

Freedom Fox, is included at the back of the booklet. It starts by asking him how the Army of God plans to stop abortions taking place. He answers: "First by disarming the murder weapons. That is by destroying the structures where the actual crimes are being committed. Second, by dis-arming the persons perpetrating the crimes by removing their hands, or at least their thumbs below the second digit." Rachelle Shannon had read her literature religiously.

In the book, group members are referred to as "termites," because they are tunneling away and undermining the buildings where abortions are performed. A long list of "thank-yous" refers to a sizeable group of people who have allegedly carried out attacks on institutions, but they are all referred to with nicknames. Freedom Fox recommends that "every Pro-Life person should commit to destroying at least one death camp, or disarming at least one baby killer." He even goes on to elaborate on his preferred methods for achieving this.

Even active "Pro-Life" campaigners have been quick to condemn the acts of violence. They believe that all life is sacred, and that by picking and choosing like the Army of God does, they would be playing God just as much as they feel the abortion clinics are. They feel intimidation is not the way to change people's minds, aside from the fact that the Army of God's activities are illegal.

A Michigan Militia training camp. Male members train their families, including children, in how to handle firearms.

THE MICHIGAN MILITIA

The Michigan Militia group is one of the growing number of US Patriot groups that are said to be home to tens of thousands of white, rightwing Americans. Experts say that all fifty US states now have organized antigovernment groups, and the cases of domestic terrorism in the USA have risen to over 900 currently on the FBI files, from approximately 100 in 1995. With the majority of these groups advocating being armed and trained in combat, the US security forces have begun to take the problem very seriously.

The Michigan Militia was started in April 1994 by Ray Southwell and his friend, the Reverend Norman Olson. Olson manages to reconcile being a Baptist minister with owning a gun store. Southwell was apparently disturbed by the liberal teaching that was going on at his child's school. The two men sought advice from a seasoned Patriot, John Trochmann, the man behind the Militia of Montana (MOM). The Michigan Militia started as a small group of like-minded men, and has now grown into one of the largest organizations of its type in America. Also known as the Wolverines, it presents a law-abiding face to outsiders. It says it doesn't condone acts of violence,

and that it works closely with local and national police forces, rather than working against them.

Despite this publicly restrained attitude, the Michigan Militia has been linked to the Oklahoma City bombing. It is known to train twice a month, fully armed, and its ex-commander, Olson, is well known for making speeches announcing the inevitability of an armed showdown with government forces.

The current commander, Lynn Van Huizen, is also the owner of a gun store in Michigan. He has gone on record as saying that he isn't "antigovernment," but he does believe that more power should be given back to the individual states, to the point where there is self-government. Most Patriots want an end to immigration, a relaxing of gun laws, and a tougher approach to education and law. They feel they could achieve this at local level without the interference of what they feel is a corrupt, communist-sympathizing federal government.

There are packs of Wolverines in 66 of Michigan's 83 counties. The groups are divided into brigades, which are clumped together in divisions. Each division is looked after by a division commander, who acts as an

THE MILITIA TRAINS TWICE A MONTH, FULLY ARMED

intermediary between individual members and the commander of the whole movement. When the group was linked to Timothy McVeigh and Terry Nichols (the two Patriots allegedly attended meetings given by the Michigan Militia), the whole organization was branded as dangerous. The FBI started to closely monitor its activities, and came to the conclusion that the two men did have some connection with the Militia group, but there was no evidence to prosecute anyone else.

In his book *Gathering Storm: America's Militia Threat*, Morris Dees makes a connection between the two killers and one of the more extreme members of the Michigan Militia, Mark Koernke. Koernke is well known in the area for his rightwing shortwave radio broadcasts where he calls himself "Mark from Michigan." He has become an unofficial spokesperson for the more extreme end of the Patriot movement, broadcasting his paranoia-filled version of politics, where he tells listeners to prepare for a "New World Order" led by the corrupt United Nations and the White House, and that the only way to protect the freedom of true Americans is to be armed and

prepared. Although Koernke denies knowing either of the bombers, the allegations that he did have led to him becoming a household name. *Time* magazine ran a seven-page article about him, and he has appeared on national television. His three videos, detailing how to prepare for the forthcoming confrontation, are selling well.

He teaches that the US government, hell bent on taking away the rights of its citizens, is secretly constructing what he calls "detention centers," and that they are already amassing UN troops ready for an invasion. Koernke, like other Patriot heroes before him, had gone into hiding at the time of writing. He was declared a federal fugitive in June 1998, but local FBI officers said there were no plans for a showdown like the disastrous one that took place at Ruby Ridge in August 1992 between federal officers and Randy Weaver, when Weaver's innocent wife and child were shot dead.

The Michigan Militia has issued public statements claiming that although Timothy McVeigh did attend some of their meetings, he found their philosophy too passive, and was eventually asked to leave because his own views were far too extreme.

115

Reverend Norman Olson in his gun store. He was Commander General of the Militia until 1995, when he was asked to resign.

FBI FIGHTS DOMESTIC TERRORISM

Even though the authorities were initially convinced the Oklahoma City bombing was carried out by international terrorists, the FBI now takes the threat of internal terrorism by Patriot groups and hate organizations very seriously. The scale of the investigations into McVeigh and Nichols revealed a whole underground network of anti-government groups, many of which have links to white supremacist organizations.

In an interview with *US News and World Report* published on December 29, 1997, a Justice Department Official said the FBI's counterterrorism budget had been nearly trebled since 1994, which in real terms meant an extra 350 agents dealing with domestic terrorism cases.

NATION OF ISLAM

Although it is controversial to label a black organization "racist," some critics have claimed that is exactly how the black power group the Nation of Islam should be defined. It is listed among the "Hatewatch" Internet pages as being a hate group, and has certainly caused a mass of publicity over the years with its sometimes extremist views on black politics. The group hasn't just been criticized by whites and Christians, it has also been dismissed by most Muslims, who believe the group shouldn't be accepted as a true part of the Islamic faith, and also by other black leaders who have distanced themselves from the more radical aspects of the group.

Despite all the controversy, the Nation of Islam is growing in popularity among the black population, mainly in the USA, but it also has a dedicated following in the UK. Its missionaries are distinctive, generally young, polite, clean-shaven men wearing neat dark suits. They present an image of self-assured power, and appeal to their brothers to join a movement based on a strong moral code, and self-empowerment. There is an emphasis on the family, women are held in high regard, and the group works hard to establish links across all sections of the black community.

It is hard to believe that a group which has such high morality and works so hard to give black politics the standing so long denied to it has been linked to, of all things, the Ku Klux Klan. However, the more extreme end of the group, including the Nation of Islam's current leader, the Honorable Minister Louis Farrakhan, believes wholeheartedly in a separatist policy. Just as the KKK believe in a single white race unadulterated by mixed-race relationships, Farrakhan believes in the black community uniting to become a powerful, God-fearing Church. Both groups believe that they are the true "chosen" race which will eventually rule the earth.

Farrakhan is an extremely controversial yet powerful

The Honorable Elijah Mohammad developed the doctrine of "Yacub's History" and led the Nation of Islam until his death in 1975.

figure. He was recruited into the organization by Malcolm X in 1955, but never followed the infamous black leader's belief in integration of both black and white populations. Malcolm X actually left the organization because of its extremist views, and although he continued to believe in the principles of Islam, he worked toward convincing the black population that race is not an issue to judge people on.

The group was born from two other organizations, the Moorish Science Temple of America, founded in 1913, and the Universal Negro Improvement Association, with the help of Wallace Dodd Ford, who added the basic Islamic principles and formed his black power group, the Nation of Islam. Ford is seen as an incarnation of Allah who came to earth to "teach the downtrodden and defenseless Black people a thorough knowledge of God and of themselves, and to put them on the road to Self-Independence with a superior culture and higher civilization than they had previously experienced." He recruited a man called Elijah Poole from Detroit and for three-and-a-half years instructed him in his divine message.

Poole was renamed the Honorable Elijah Muhammad, and Allah revealed the true history of humanity's creation and civilization of the planet to him.

When the Master (Ford) departed in 1934, Elijah Muhammad began spreading the word. He told potential converts about "Yacub's History," how the moon had divided from the earth, and the moon people, who were black, were the first people to populate the new planet, starting with Mecca. A team of scientists was in charge of civilization, but one called Yacub decided to cause trouble. He was expelled to the remote island of Patmos, where he put his scientific knowledge to good use and in revenge created a race of devils, all of whom were pale-skinned. When the white devils finally populated the mainland, they caused trouble by setting the blacks

116

The Million Man March in Washington DC, 1995, was organized by Louis Farrakhan as a show of the strength of black power.

MALCOLM X

Malcolm Little was one of eight children born to a radical Baptist minister and his wife. Malcolm's father was murdered when the boy was six, allegedly after being warned off by the Ku Klux Klan. Malcolm's mother was devastated, and all the children were eventually taken into state care when she couldn't cope any more. After being in various institutions, Malcolm turned to a life of crime in Harlem until he was imprisoned in 1946 for burglary offences. It was while he was serving his time that he became interested in the teachings of Elijah Muhammad.

He was released six years later, and joined the Nation of Islam, quickly becoming one of its leading lights and most popular figures.

He adopted the name Malcolm X (the X is a symbol of separation), married, and had six daughters. His beliefs were initially at the extreme edge of black politics and he was known for his charismatic speeches. He famously told Alex Haley in a *Playboy* interview published in May 1963: "I don't know when Armageddon is supposed to be. But I know that the time is near when the white man will be finished. The signs are all around us."

Malcolm X fell out with the Nation of Islam leaders in 1964. He also made a historic trip to Mecca, where he was so impressed with the Muslim way of life that he renounced all his separatist teachings and began preaching that black and white should work together for the good of humanity generally. On February 21, 1965, he was addressing a crowd of about 400 people when he was murdered in front of his family. It is thought that the murder was linked to the Nation of Islam, although the group has always strongly denied this.

The Nation of Islam newspaper is sold on street corners to fund Farrakhan's projects.

118

THE FARRAKHAN MURDER PLOT

Events took a twist in the continuing conspiracy theory surrounding the assassination of Malcolm X and the involvement of the Nation of Islam, when in 1996, one of Malcolm X's daughters was alleged to have masterminded a plan to murder Louis Farrakhan, the black supremacist group's leader.

According to the FBI, Qubilah Shabazz, who saw her father being shot dead, was alleged to have plotted to have Farrakhan killed because she suspected him of being involved in her father's murder. The whole case rested on the testimony of an FBI informant, well known for infiltrating groups that cause problems for the government. Supporters of Shabazz said the whole case was ridiculous, and even Farrakhan accused the FBI of trying to make trouble between his group and the family of Malcolm X.

Malcolm X's wife, Betty, went on record as saying she was suspicious of the group's involvement. *The New York Post* then took up the story, which led to a huge lawsuit being issued by the Nation of Islam for libel. The confusion still continues, with accounts of the infamous black leader's death, and his daughter's subsequent troubles, varying from source to source.

WHITES WOULD RULE UNTIL JUDGMENT DAY, WHEN BLACKS WOULD RISE UP

against each other. The whites would rule for 6,000 years until Judgment Day, when the blacks would rise up and forever rule the earth. In some versions of the story, the white devils are wiped out forever.

When Elijah Muhammad, who is still revered as a prophet, contrary to Islamic teachings, died in 1975, internal squabbles caused confusion within the group. Eventually, Muhammad's son Wallace gained control, but his views differed from his father's. He changed the group's name to the World Community of Al-Islam in the West, and then the Muslim Community of America, and tried to maneuver his followers to more mainstream Islamic teachings. He followed Malcolm X's

later example and teachings, preaching integration rather than separation, and emphasized the importance of traditional Muslim life. Members didn't smoke, drink alcohol, take drugs, or attend dances. The group was eventually dissolved, partly because Wallace felt it should be fully integrated into the world-wide Muslim movement, and partly due to financial complications.

Farrakhan resurrected the movement, its name, and its extreme beliefs in 1977, and has maintained a tight grip on the group's affairs. His early rallying speeches often contained anti-Semitic and racist ideology, yet he is seen as the most powerful black leader in America today. The group now tries to portray a more restrained view of society, but in reality still holds its separatist beliefs.

Farrakhan has been extremely successful in helping the poorer black communities, not only with the huge

***R**ight: Activists attend the public enquiry into the murder of black London teenager Stephen Lawrence. Five white youths were charged, but never convicted.*

NATION OF ISLAM MEETS GADDAFI

On August 31, 1996, Louis Farrakhan, leader of the Nation of Islam (or Black Muslims) accepted the Gaddafi Award for international humanitarian achievement in Tripoli, Libya, sparking fierce criticism of the black leader's ideology. The award was accompanied by a $250,000 "contribution" to his works, but Farrakhan had to refuse the money because the US government would not allow him or his group to be funded by "dictators." He told the assembled dignitaries: "While I accept the honor of the prize, I will ask you to hold the money until this matter is decided in a court of law."

Reports in the Libyan press also spoke of a $1 billion "gift" from the government of Libya to be used to help the Nation of Islam's program of "reform and spiritual and economic development of the black community in the US."

Farrakhan issued an angry statement aimed at the US government, saying there was no reason why he should not be allowed to accept the money from his Muslim "brother," and challenged the US authorities to match the generous gift with the aim of getting the black homeless off the streets, start drug rehabilitation centers, set up businesses, and give the black man back his pride.

On his return from the Middle East, Farrakhan made speeches to his loyal followers, who number in their thousands. He said he wasn't an enemy of America, but that it was time for a "showdown."

HIS IDEOLOGY OF GIVING BROTHERS BACK THEIR PRIDE HAS PROVEN MASSIVELY POPULAR

problems of drugs and criminal activities, but also by instigating ambitious self-help projects. His ideology of giving brothers back their pride has proven massively popular. He has initiated businesses, bought land, and started farming communities. Money is usually raised through small donations or subscriptions to the Nation's newspaper *The Final Call*. He has also been berated for fundraising activities connected to various countries that the US government would describe as "hostile," but Farrakhan believes money given from Muslim countries is in effect a gift from Allah.

A movement that offers something genuinely positive from life has proved extremely popular, especially with America's disaffected young black men. The Nation of Islam now has 50,000–150,000 followers, and the movement is growing, even though there is continued controversy surrounding its politics. Despite the fact that the group is neither embraced by the mainstream Islamic community nor major black role models in the US, because it is seen as too extreme, Farrakhan is a leading light in US black politics today.

BIBLIOGRAPHY

Baigent, Michael, Leigh, Richard and Lincoln, Henry, *The Messianic Legacy*, Arrow, 1996

Barrett, David V., *Sects, Cults and Alternative Religions: A World Survey and Sourcebook*, Blandford, 1996

Beit-Hallahmi, Benjamin, *The Illustrated Encyclopedia of Active New Religions, Sects and Cults*, Rosen Publishing, 1993

Brookesmith, Peter (ed.), *The Occult Connection: The Ways in Which Man has Tried to Make Sense of His Universe*, Black Cat, 1984

Christie-Murray, David, *A History of Heresy*, New English Library, 1976

Dees, Morris and Corcoran, James, *Gathering Storm: America's Militia Threat*, HarperPerennial, 1997

Elliott, Paul, *Warrior Cults: A History of Magical, Mystical and Murderous Organisations*, Blandford, 1996

Green, Miranda J., *Exploring the World of the Druids*, Thames and Hudson, 1997

Hassan, Steven, *Combatting Cult Mind Control: Protection, Rescue and Recovery from Destructive Cults*, Aquarian Press, 1988

Hinnells, John R. (ed.), *The Penguin Dictionary of Religions*, Penguin, 1984

Jordan, Michael, *Cults: Prophecies, Practices and Personalities*, Michael Jordan, 1996

Kaplan, David E. and Marshall, Andrew, *The Cult at the End of the World: The Incredible Story of AUM*, Arrow, 1997

King, Martin and Breault, Marc, *Preacher of Death: The Shocking Inside Story of David Koresh and the Waco Seige*, Signet, 1993

Knight, Stephen, *The Brotherhood: The Explosive Exposé of the Secret World of the Freemasons*, Panther, 1985

Lane, Brian, *The Encyclopedia of Occult and Supernatural Murder*, Headline, 1995

Langley, Myrtle, Butterworth, John and Allan, John, *A Book of Beliefs: Religions, New Faiths, the Paranormal*, Lion, 1985

Larson, Bob, *Larson's New Book of Cults*, Tyndale House, 1989

Linedecker, Clifford L., *Massacre at Waco: The Shocking True Story of Cult Leader David Koresh and the Branch Davidians*, Virgin, 1993

Martin, Walter, *The Kingdom of the Cults*, Bethany House, 1992

Mizell Jr, Louis R., *Target USA: The Inside Story of the New Terrorist War*, John Wiley and Sons, 1998

Parrinder, Geoffrey, *The World's Living Religions*, Pan, 1977

Porterfield, Kay Marie, *Straight Talk About Cults*, Facts on File, 1995

Ritchie, Jean, *The Secret World of Cults: Inside the Sects That Take Over Lives*, Angus and Robertson, 1991

Saliba, John A., *Perspectives on New Religious Movements*, Geoffrey Chapman, 1995

Shaw, William, *Spying in Guru Land: Inside Britain's Cults*, Fourth Estate, 1995

Smart, Ninian, *The World's Religions*, Cambridge University Press, 1995

Steiger, Brad and Hewes, Hayden, *Inside Heaven's Gate*, Signet, 1997

Stern, Kenneth S., *A Force Upon the Plain: The American Militia Movement and the Politics of Hate*, Simon and Schuster, 1996

Thackrah, John Richard, *Encyclopedia of Terrorism and Political Violence*, Routledge and Kegan Paul, 1987

Van Helsing, Jan, *Secret Societies and their Power in the 20th Century*, Ewertverlag SL, 1993

Various authors, *Serial Murderers: Index*, Marshall Cavandish, 1995

INDEX

123

PICTURE CREDITS

The publisher would like to thank the following agencies and individuals who have supplied photographs for this book.

Key: l = left; r = right; t = top; b = bottom; c = center

Front cover: B. Charlon/L'Express/Camera Press. Back cover: Les Stone/Sygma (l); R. J. Davis/Camera Press (r). **Title page:** Popperfoto/Reuters (l); Images Colour Library (r). **Contents:** Fortean Picture Library (tl); Les Stone/Sygma (tr); Epix/Sygma (cl); The Aetherius Society (cr); John van Hasselt/Sygma (bl); Lynn Pelham/Camera Press (br). **Introduction:** 10l Fortean Picture Library; 10r Images Colour Library; 11l Popperfoto; 11r Ethan Hoffman/Camera Press.

Chapter One

12 R. J. Davis/Camera Press; 13 Images Colour Library; 14 Fortean Picture Library; 15t, 15b Images Colour Library; 16 Fortean Picture Library; 17l AKG; 17r Images Colour Library; 18, 19l, 19r, 20, 21r Images Colour Library; 21l Ancient Art & Architecture Collection; 22 Images Colour Library; 23tl Mary Evans Picture Library; 23tr Images Colour Library; 23br Stewart Mark/Fairlady/Camera Press; 24 Abbas/Magnum; 25tl, 25tr, 25cl Mary Evans Picture Library; 25br Photo News/Gamma/Frank Spooner; 26 R. J. Davis/Camera Press; 27l Mary Evans Picture Library; 27r Images Colour Library.

Chapter Two

28l Ethan Hoffman/Camera Press; 29 Gideon Mendel/Network; 30 AKG; 31l Vince Streano/Topham Picturepoint; 31tr Hulton Getty; 31bl PA News; 32l Bridgeman Art Library; 32r Images Colour Library; 33 Padraig O'Donnell/Camera Press; 34 C. K. Kim/Camera Press; 35 Les Stone/Sygma; 36l Owen Franken/Sygma; 36r, 37, Popperfoto/Reuters; 38 Ralph Perry/Black Star/Colorific; 39t B. Charlon/L'Express/Camera Press; 39b Rene Burri/Magnum; 40 Nutan/Rapho/Network; 41 PA News; 42 A. Hall/Frank Spooner; 43l Dilip Mehta/Colorific; 43tr AKG London/Associated Press; 43b Dilip Mehta/Colorific; 44 Lionel Cherruault/Camera Press; 45l A. Tannenbaum/Sygma; 45r Ethan Hoffman/Camera Press; 46 Nikita Blikov/Camera Press; 47 R. Martinez/G. Regerat/Sygma.

Chapter Three

48 Images Colour Library; 49 Petar Petrov/Popperfoto/Reuters; 50–51 Aetherius Society; 52 Images Colour Library; 53 Sygma; 54r, 54l International Raelian Movement; 55 Stewart Ferguson/Camera Press; 56 Jean-François Cyr/International Raelian Movement; 57l, 57r International Raelian Movement; 58t A. Tannenbaum/Sygma; 58b A Koester/Sygma; 59 A. Koester/Soqui/Sygma; 60t Gamma/Liaison/Frank Spooner; 60l Spragg/Sygma; 60r A. Tannenbaum/ Sygma; 61 Sygma; 62, 63tr, 63c Unarius Academy of Science; 63b Mark Graham/Sygma; 64l, 64r, 65r One World Family Commune; 65l Topham Picturepoint.

Chapter Four

66 Waco Tribune Herald/Sygma; 67 Associated Press; 68 Le Soleil/Sygma; 69t, 69l Sygma; 69r Le Journal de Montreal/Sygma; 70t Luigi Baldelli Contrasto/Katz Pictures; 70b Sygma; 71 Sipa Press/Rex Features; 72 Shizuo Kambayashi/Associated Press; 73 Epix/Sygma; 74l Pagnotta Dafonseca/Katz Pictures; 74r Tokyo Shimbun/Sygma; 75t Kimimasa Mayama/Popperfoto/Reuters; 75b Kyodo News/Associated Press; 76 Popperfoto; 77r Elizabeth Baranyai/Sygma; 77l Waco Tribune Herald/Sygma; 78 Rod Aydelotte/Waco Tribune Herald/Sygma; 79l Smith/Saba/Rea/Katz Pictures; 79r Dunleavy/San Antonio Express News/Sygma; 80 P. Ledru/Sygma; 81l San Francisco Examiner/Associated Press; 81r, 82 Associated Press; 83 P. Ledru/Sygma; 85l Rick Browne/LA Times; 85r Mark Boster/LA Times; 85c Popperfoto/Reuters.

Chapter Five

86 Images Colour Library; 87 Lynn Pelham/Camera Press; 88l AKG; 88r Erich Kocian/Camera Press; 89t Popperfoto; 89b Rex Features; 90t, 90r Popperfoto; 90l Popperfoto/Reuters; 91l Rex Features; 91r Associated Press/Topham Picturepoint; 92 Martyn Goddard/Colorific; 93 Howard C. Moore/Deseret News; 94 © Chuck Fadely/Miami Herald; 95tr, 95bl © Tim Chapman/Miami Herald; 95c © Albert Coya/Miami Herald; 96l Hulton Getty; 96r Images Colour Library; 97t Aron Paramor; 97b Images Colour Library; 98t Cheetham/Magnum; 98b David Stout/Sygma; 99 Popperfoto; 100 John Reardon/Katz Pictures; 101l Lynn Pelham/Camera Press; 101r Danny Lyon/Magnum; 102 Lynn Pelham/Camera Press; 103t, 103b AKG; 104 Nicolas Jallot/Gamma/Frank Spooner; 105l, 105tr, 105cr Les Stone/Sygma.

Chapter Six

106 Gamma/Frank Spooner; 107 Paul Hackett/Popperfoto/Reuters; 108l Popperfoto/Reuters; 108r David Modell/Katz Pictures; 109l Lawrence Merville/Gamma/ Liaison/Frank Spooner; 109r Associated Press/Topham Picturepoint; 110, 111tr Robert Kirkham/Buffalo News; 111bl The Forum of Fargo; 112l Popperfoto/Reuters; 112r Erik Lesser/Gamma/Liaison/ Frank Spooner; 113l Blake Sell/Popperfoto/Reuters; 113r Popperfoto/Reuters; 114 C. Howe/Sygma; 115tr Hernandez/Grand Rapids Press/Gamma/Liaison/Frank Spooner; 115l Muskegomchron/Gamma/Liaison/Frank Spooner; 115br Topham Picturepoint; 116 Archive Photos; 117tl A. Tannenbaum/Sygma; 117tr Sion Touhig/Sygma; 117b Ted Russell/Sygma; 118l John van Hasselt/Sygma; 118r Mike Segar/Popperfoto/Reuters; 119l Peter Morgan/Popperfoto/Reuters; 119r Paul Hackett/Popperfoto/Reuters.

124